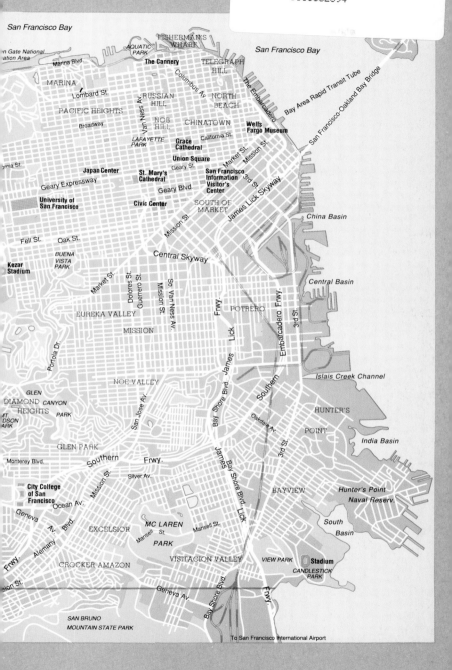

C000002594

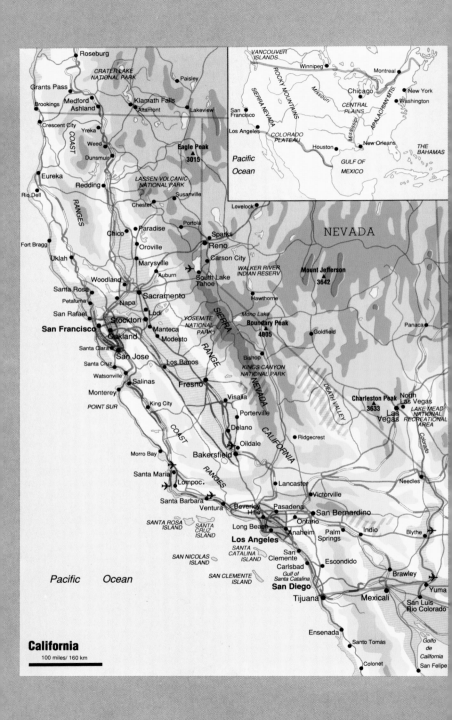

California

100 miles/ 160 km

San FRANCISCO

Written and Presented by **Ann Cherian**

Anne Cherian

INSIGHT *POCKET* GUIDES

Insight Pocket Guide:

SAN FRANCISCO

Directed by
Hans Höfer

Managing Editor
Martha Ellen Zenfell

Photography by
David Ryan

Design Concept by
V Barl

Design by
Klaus Geisler

© 1993 APA Publications (HK) Ltd

All Rights Reserved

Printed in Singapore by
Höfer Press (Pte) Ltd
Fax: 65-8616438

Distributed in the United States by
Houghton Mifflin Company
2 Park Street
Boston, Massachusetts 02108
ISBN: 0-395-66912-X

Distributed in Canada by
Thomas Allen & Son
390 Steelcase Road East
Markham, Ontario L3R 1G2
ISBN: 0-395-66912-X

Distributed in the UK & Ireland by
GeoCenter International UK Ltd
The Viables Center, Harrow Way
Basingstoke, Hampshire RG22 4BJ
ISBN: 9-62421-504-9

Worldwide distribution enquiries:
Höfer Communications Pte Ltd
38 Joo Koon Road
Singapore 2262
ISBN: 9-62421-504-9

NO part of this book may be reproduced,
stored in a retrieval system or transmitted in any form
or means electronic, mechanical, photocopying,
recording or otherwise, without prior written permis-
sion of Apa Publications. Brief text quotations with use
of photographs are exempted for book review purposes
only.
As every effort is made to provide accurate information
in this publication, we would appreciate it if readers
would call our attention to any errors that may occur by
communicating with Apa Villa, 81 The Cut, London
SE1 8LL. Tel: 71-620-0008, Fax: 71-620-1074.
Information has been obtained from sources believed
to be reliable, but its accuracy and completeness,
and the opinions based thereon, are not guaranteed.

Welcome!

Welcome! Long before I moved to the Bay Area and settled in Berkeley, just across the bay from San Francisco, my mother told me stories about the city: of driving across the newly-opened Bay Bridge with her uncle while cars all around were honking because he absolutely refused to go fast; of putting on silk stockings, gloves and a hat before going into 'the city', as she always called it.

Today's San Francisco is rather different. There are still the old places – like Tadich's which still has the best seafood around and Golden Gate Park – but I certainly don't wear gloves except when it's very cold, and a slow-moving car in the 1990s is likely to be pulled over and given a ticket.

In *Insight Pocket Guide: San Francisco* I have tried to show all the different sides of the city in a series of tailor-made, tried and tested itineraries. As in all Insight Pocket Guides, itineraries are intended for the active and inquisitive traveler who wants to extract the optimum pleasure out of a brief visit. Consequently, I start with four full-day itineraries encompassing what I consider are San Francisco's essential, must-see sights – the Golden Gate Bridge, 49-Mile Drive, Chinatown and Alcatraz – followed by Pick & Choose options (divided into morning and afternoon tours) to suit a variety of interests and tastes. Finally, for those with more time, come a series of full-day trips beyond the city, such as hot-air ballooning over Napa Valley vineyards, and a choice of weekend excursions, including trips to Yosemite National Park and Lake Tahoe. Each itinerary includes step-by-step directions and my personal recommendations on where to eat, drink and lodge.

Supporting the itineraries are sections on history and culture, shopping and food, and at the back you will find a Practical Information section supplying essential tips. My hope is that you find *Insight Pocket Guide: San Francisco* a catalyst as much as an invaluable guide. **Welcome! — Anne Cherian**

Contents

Preceding pages:
city and bay

What to Know

Maps

9

Following pages:
San Francisco's famous cable cars

HOTEL
LIVE
COIN GALLERY of SAN FRANCISCO Inc.
Since 1949
RARE COINS STAMPS OBJECTS D'ART
POWELL & MARKET to BEACH & HYDE WASHINGTON & JACKSON
1

HISTORY

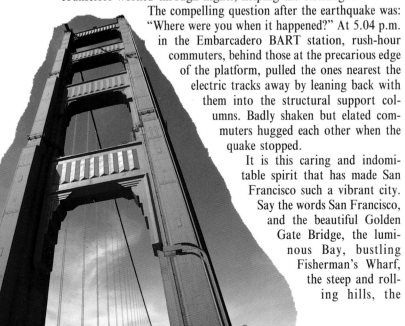

The earthquake on 17 October 1989 placed San Francisco on the map as the city of flames and fighters. Suddenly the world knew about the San Andreas Fault and memories of the 1906 catastrophe were resurrected.

TV screens around the world blazed with the fallen Bay Bridge, the burning Marina, and the crushing collapse of the Nimitz freeway. Many thought the city devastated.

In fact, it came through mostly intact. The death toll was far below early estimates of hundreds, while most buildings rocked, but did not actually crash.

Left out of the media's eager coverage of the catastrophe however, were dauntless San Franciscans: ties unknotted, sleeves rolled, grimy but determined residents stood at intersections, calmly directing traffic with flashlights; companies such as Levi Strauss, called each one of their employees to verify that their families were all right; and counselors worked through nights, helping the distraught.

The compelling question after the earthquake was: "Where were you when it happened?" At 5.04 p.m. in the Embarcadero BART station, rush-hour commuters, behind those at the precarious edge of the platform, pulled the ones nearest the electric tracks away by leaning back with them into the structural support columns. Badly shaken but elated commuters hugged each other when the quake stopped.

It is this caring and indomitable spirit that has made San Francisco such a vibrant city. Say the words San Francisco, and the beautiful Golden Gate Bridge, the luminous Bay, bustling Fisherman's Wharf, the steep and rolling hills, the

Culture

eclectic architecture and the parks will come to mind. But long before the city became what it is today, long before the fault line became newsworthy, there were the people of San Francisco.

San Francisco is the story of a people determined to live in an incomparably beautiful environment despite the threat of destruction. Their spirit and love of life has been proven over and over. It was there after the 1906 earthquake, when in less than a week plans for the first new downtown building were published. And it was warm and buoyant as ever, way back in the Gold Rush days of the 1850s, when citizens bowed before his highness, "Emperor Norton I," really Joshua Abraham Norton, English merchant, who sported a beaver hat with three brightly colored feathers.

Joshua A. Norton came to San Francisco in 1849. Within four years his Midas touch had garnered him a fortune in real estate. He was so rich and knowledgeable that he was fondly called the "Emperor." Norton resisted that name, and drew attention to the greatness of American democracy. One day he embarked on an ambitious project to corner the world's rice markets. The Norton Rice Market became famous, but when backers lost their investments, the "Emperor" turned "pauper" and disappeared. Just when people were beginning to forget about him, he strode down Montgomery Street wearing a part army, part navy uniform, went straight to the office of the *Bulletin* and put in an announcement proclaiming himself "Norton I, Emperor of the United States and Protector of Mexico."

For the next 26 years the Emperor used his own royal currency, "cash certificates" made for him by a friendly printer, honored by every merchant in the city. He took his duties seriously, sending cablegrams to Queen Victoria, the Czar and the Kaiser. He established the tradition of the public Christmas tree at Union Square.

He died in 1880. Flags were flown at half-mast and about 30,000

Chinatown Gate

people followed the funeral cortege to the grave of a wealthy pioneer. In 1934, the Pacific Union Club moved Norton's remains to Woodlawn Cemetery. It was a day of pomp San Francisco style; the mayor gave a speech, the band played, a military salute was fired and *Taps* sounded from the hilltop.

The gold-seekers are now part of the city's capricious history, but the warmth of San Francisco remains. Visitors always remark on the friendliness of the inhabitants; they return repeatedly to San Francisco, explaining that it is the people who make the city attractive. Indeed, San Francisco has had a long bohemian history of assimilating visitors, immigrants and non-conformists, and Emperor Norton is just one instance of the latter.

Look around San Francisco. The people who call the city "home" are diverse: Chinese, Japanese, Italians, Mexicans, descendants of the rip-roaring Gold Rush days, in fascinating Chinatown, Japantown and North Beach enclaves.

But San Francisco does not just absorb immigrants. The city has hosted various bohemian, and sometimes violent, minorities within the United States. After World War II, a defiant wave of artists, intellectuals and dissatisfied New Yorkers, refusing to adapt to the prevailing sober after-war mentality of save-for-a-rainy-day, found a flourishing and variegated non-conformist community in San Francisco. The Beat generation, in the 1950s, set their hearts on North Beach, making it a kind of easy-come-and-go haunt, where their "I-don't-care-I-don't-know-and-it-doesn't-make-a-difference" sentiment met with empathy.

A decade of political activism began in 1960 when students protested a City Hall hearing of the House UnAmerican Activities Committee. Six years later, the so-called hippie community took clear form in the Haight-Ashbury District. Ideologically, the hippies were younger brothers and sisters of the Beats. They admired the same poets and philosophers and shared an existentialist lifestyle. The real-life hero of several Jack Kerouac novels, Neal Cassady, appeared on the hippie scene. Hippies embraced pacifism and their erotic attitudes — as summarized by the slogan "If It Moves, Stroke It" — helped bring local acceptance of gay and bisexual practices and the opening here later of a "gay mecca."

Mind-drugs like LSD, marijuana and others became staple diets, and psychedelia was born. Hippies all over the US moved to the Haight-Ashbury district, a run-down but hitherto respectable area of Victorian houses. Indian fabrics, mirrors and chimes decorated the houses in the neighborhood. In 1967, the "Summer of Love" was held in the Haight.

Perhaps it is no wonder, then, that today San Francisco is the gay capital of the world. Just as the beatniks sank their roots into North Beach and the hippies the Haight, the gays took over the Tenderloin District, Folsom Street and the Castro. Large numbers of gays disembarked in San Francisco during World War II, when the US army started a rigorous weeding out of homosexuals. Many stayed, being the first time in a place where their sheer volume made it easy to congregate without embarrassment. In 1969, the gay rebellion took the US by storm. A police raid in a New York gay bar became a riot that started a civil rights movement across the United States. The Castro became active central campaign grounds. In 1977 came a breakthrough, when Harvey Milk became the first gay elected to the Board of Supervisors, the equivalent of a city council. Sadly, Milk was gunned down and killed by a political opponent less than a year after his inauguration.

Today the gays continue to be a vocal and active presence in the city. San Franciscans tread, and often cross, the fine line between gathering someone in but also letting him be. It is this singular trait which contributes to the vibrant spirit of San Francisco, and which accounts for the spontaneous reaction to, and acceptance of, change. President Bush proclaimed the fortitude and spontaneous caring he saw in San Francisco after the quake "the American way." But citizens feel that it is the "San Franciscan way."

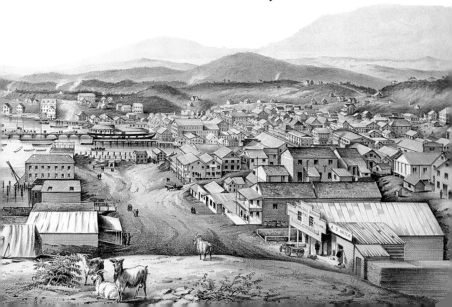

Historical Outline

1000 B.C: Indians who revere the earth strive for a society in harmony with the physical environment in the area known today as San Francisco.

1770s: The Spanish government founds a Presidio (garrison) and mission peacefully near the San Francisco Bay Area.

1820s: Mexico breaks away from Spain. In 1824, the Mexican Congress promises security to law-abiding foreign settlers. American and English businessmen begin a gradual influx. Richardson, an Englishman, is widely acknowledged as the person who founds Yerba Buena, the town preceding San Francisco.

1846: The US captures California at Monterey and the American flag is soon flying in Yerba Buena. In 1847, it is renamed San Francisco by the American settlers.

1848: Gold is discovered in Coloma, setting off the Gold Rush. Fortune hunters pour in. 30,000 from mainland US by covered wagons, 40,000 sail from Europe, Australia, South America and China, and 9,000 Mexicans join the torrent. Prices of food and lodging reach incredible heights. The most money is made, not by miners, but by shopkeepers – who sell eggs at $1 each – and landlords.

Brothels, opium dens and general lawlessness become rampant. Criminals from the Sydney penal colony start arriving.

1850s: California is admitted to the Union. Gold yields start to decline. In 1859, the present city seal is adopted. The Comstock Lode, a rich vein of silver, injects a second boost to the economy, turning it from a prosperous frontier town into a metropolis.

1860s: The Chinese population grows rapidly. Immigrants come intially to mine, but their success brings resentment, and they are sent away from the richest veins. 9,000 Chinese are brought in to build railroads. The Chinese with their underground gambling and opium dens cause racist federal laws stopping immigration to be passed in the 1880s and 1890s.

1870s: Rich businessmen, lawyers and speculators who profit from the mines live and entertain in high style on Nob Hill, creating a different class of citizens from the rough fortune hunters of the old pioneer town. On April 4, 1870, Golden Gate Park is established.

1873: The world's first cable car runs between Kearny and Jones streets. In the late 1880s, cable cars transport more than 75,000 people a month.

1880s: Railroad magnates defy the law with bribes and payoffs. Cultural life nevertheless flourishes with California State and San Francisco universities, public and private libraries, 12 theaters and an opera at the Tivoli. Numerous newspapers are published. In 1887, the *San Francisco Examiner* is given to William R. Hearst by his father.

1906: The famous earthquake destroys the central business district, Nob Hill and Chinatown. Reconstruction soon begins on an enormous scale.

World War I boosts mining, manufacturing and agriculture. Abundant oil reserves are mined. The economy is buoyant.

1936: The Oakland Bay Bridge opens in November, followed by the Golden Gate Bridge six months later to an uproarious reception.

1945: The San Francisco Conference, formally known as the United Nations Conference on International Organization, establishes the United Nations. 50 members sign the Charter of the United Nations.

World War II sees the influx of more than 500,000 workers in response to new industries in the Bay area, in addition to thousands of soldiers passing through to the war in the Pacific or stationed around the Bay. Many people remain after the war, contributing to an already flourishing economy.

Japanese-Americans are incarcerated and sent to mass concentration camps.

1951: Prime Minister Yoshida of Japan signs the treaty ending World War II at Opera House.

1950s: Counter-culture groups across the US congregate in the city, attracted by its bohemian non-conformity. The beatniks take over North Beach.

1960s: The hippies claim Haight-Ashbury, but soon relinquish the area to unruly down-and-outers, street gangs and criminals.

1969: Gays become predominant in the Tenderloin District, Folsom Street and the Castro.

1974: The BART (Bay Area Rapid Transit System) starts a regular transbay service, linking metropolitan stations around the Bay.

1975: Active campaigns for gay rights start in the Castro. In 1977, Harvey Milk becomes the first gay to be elected to the Board of Supervisors, the equivalent of a city council. Harvey Milk was assassinated along with Mayor George Moscone by a political opponent.

1989: An earthquake measuring 7.1 on the Richter Scale shocks the city. A segment of the Bay Bridge collapses and fire rages in the Marina area.

The following four days have been planned for those who want to see and do as much as possible in a short time. You are encouraged to deviate from these itineraries should you see anything interesting and come back to them later. Try to make the most of your time in a place Katherine Amos Taylor called **"The City of Romance and the Gateway to Adventure."**

NB. Please call the restaurants to make reservations and to ensure that they are open. Should a restaurant be booked or closed, refer to the "Dining Experiences" section and pick another one. For your convenience I have listed them by their specialities. The price gauge for all restaurants is also found in that section.

The price indications of recommended meals in the Day Itineraries are: $ = less than \$10; $$ = more than \$10; $$$ = more than \$20.

Cable Cars and Golden Gate Bridge

Breakfast at Campton Place Kempinski ($$); cable car ride; Fisherman's Wharf; walk across the Golden Gate Bridge; tea at Bridgeway Café in Sausalito; ferry back to Fisherman's Wharf;

Powell Street cable car

dinner at Square One Restaurant ($$$); drink at the Top of the Mark.

Things to do before: call Campton Place Kempinski at 781-5155 to make breakfast reservations; call Square One at 788-1110 to make dinner reservations.

Going on walks in any city is one way of getting to know it better. It is tantamount to signing your name on a freshly-cemented sidewalk. As Keats said, "Touch has a memory".

On your first day, put on a pair of comfortable, sturdy walking shoes and bring a warm jacket and your camera.

Begin your day like a number of select San Franciscans: have breakfast at **Campton Place Kempinski** (340 Stockton Street, between Sutter and Post). Its old-world elegance and impeccable service promise a tranquil start to your day. Although it is a major hotel and caters primarily to visitors, Campton Place has developed a core clientele of local breakfast regulars. Get there by 9 a.m. to ensure a place if you did not make reservations. The food is traditional with unusual touches: buttermilk waffles with almond butter, and maybe even huckleberry gingerbread pancakes.

At about 10 a.m. stroll down to the cable car stop at **Post and Powell streets**. Just before it arrives you will hear the tracks singing and feel the vibrations. Developed by Andrew Smith Hallidie in 1873 – he gripped the wheel of the world's first cable car and roared down Clay Street at an

CABLE CAR TICKETS

BUY
TICKET
BEFORE
BOARDING
CABLE
CAR

Tickets good for approximately
2 hours from time of purchase.

exhilarating four miles (6½ km) per hour –
cable cars were made a national landmark
on 1 October, 1964. The fare is $2 and the
cars are usually crowded.

If you feel you cannot fight the crowds,
just walk another four blocks to **Powell
and Market** and queue. Buy your ticket
from the self-service ticket machine. This is
the **Powell-Mason Line** and you will ride to
one of two terminals.

Be careful to hold on tight during the
ride and when you get off, continue walking
on Taylor in the same direction. Three
blocks later you will be in the hubbub of
Fisherman's Wharf.

If you plan to take another cable car ride
during your stay in San Francisco, the
shortest wait is at **California and Van Ness**. You will also get a
wonderful view of the bay along the way since the car toils up opulent
Nob Hill before depositing passengers at the **Embarcadero**, in the
heart of the **Financial District**.

Fisherman's Wharf, along with the Golden Gate Bridge, represents
San Francisco to most people. Decades ago this was the center of a
huge fishing industry. You can still find remnants of those times, but
today the wharf fishes for other goods: visitors. Indeed most San
Franciscans regard the Wharf as less theirs than the province of the
tourists. It is usually mobbed but full of color and activity. **Only in
San Francisco** (AO-1), sells maps of the city. The area from **Pier 39
to Ghirardelli Square** is popular for shopping. During spring and
summer vibrant and eye-catching flowers are everywhere. You cannot
miss them, clustered tightly in large pots at Pier 39 and neatly
arranged in rows outside.

The **ships** are the other big draw at Fisherman's Wharf. The USS
Pampanito, docked at Pier 45, can be seen for the price of a ticket.
This 312-feet (95-meter) submarine was built in 1943 and played a
major role in World War II. Further on at the foot of **Hyde Street**
is the *Balclutha*, a steel-hulled square-rigged vessel built in Scotland
in 1886. This vessel is the last survivor of the Cape Horn fleet.

Beyond such suggestions, there is no set pattern to your first
morning in San Francisco. Do as you please. But remember, you will
be doing a fair amount of walking later so don't tire yourself. When
you get hungry, wander through the
many restaurants and stop if something
tickles your taste buds. During **crab season** (mid-November to June) people from all
over the city and the world line up for fresh
Dungeness crab and a loaf of sourdough bread,
the quintessential taste of San Francisco. If the

Figurehead on the *Balclutha* **20**

Day I: Morning

0,3 miles / 500 m

Historic Ships

Pier 39

FISHERMAN'S WHARF

The Embarcadero

Beach St.

The Cannery

Ghiradelli Square

The Anchorage

Bay St.

Taylor St.

Mason St.

Powell St.

Hyde St.

Leavenworth St.

Columbus Av.

Lombard St.

TELEGRAPH HILL

Coit Tower

Grant Av.

Larkin St.

Fibert St.

NORTH BEACH

Green St.

RUSSIAN HILL

Broadway Green St.

Square One

Pacific Av.

Sidney Walton Park

Embarcadero

Ferry Builing

Polk St.

Pacific Av.

Jackson Square

Washington St.

Chinese Culture Center

Embarcadero Center

Sacramento St.

Justin Hermann Plaza

Embarcadero Freeway

Washington St.

NOB HILL

CHINATOWN

Wells Fargo Museum

California St.

Sacramento St.

California St.

Top of The Mark

Chinatown Gateway

Stock Exchange

Fremont St.

Bush St.

Campton Place

Grant Av.

Crocker Galleria

Cable Car Stop

Mason St.

Post St.

Hotel Kempinski

Geary St.

Union Square

O'Farrell St.

Market St.

Mission St.

4th St.

Moscone Convention Center

Folsom St.

Van Ness Av.

Polk St.

Larkin St.

Hyde St.

Leavenworth St.

Taylor St.

San Francisco Visitor Information Center

Golden Gate Av.

SOUTH OF MARKET

6th St.

Museum of Modern Art

Civic Center

Opera House

8th St.

Harrison St.

Brannan St.

Tiburon Blvd.

Trestle Glen Blvd.

Paradise Dr.

PARADISE BEACH COUNTY PARK

RICHARDSON BAY PARK

TIBURON

Tiburon Blvd

TIBURON UPLANDS NATURE PRESERVE

Richardson

Belvedere Av.

E. San Rafael Av.

Tiburon Ferry Terminal

Racoon

Bay

MARINSHIP PARK

Strait

Bridgeway

Sausalito Ferry Terminal

SAUSALITO 1/101

GOLDEN GATE NATIONAL RECREATION AREA

Bunker Rd.

Fort Baker

San Francisco Bay

Golden Gate Bridge

Day I

weather is clement you can eat out, or you can sit in a glassy restaurant and watch the lapping waves.

Boats are always moored here and if you are interested you can take down the numbers of those that offer day fishing trips. Should you get tired of the Wharf, walk towards the **Cannery** and on to **Ghirardelli Square**. The water on your right and a large red brick building will tell you that you have found the place. The cannery used to be the Del Monte fruit packing plant and has a number of shops, gourmet markets, restaurants and art galleries. Ghirardelli Square was named after Domingo Ghirardelli, an Italian merchant who came to

San Francisco in 1849. He set up a successful chocolate business and built this complex between 1900 and 1916. Since then the 15-feet (4½ -meter) illuminated sign has been a familiar sight for those at sea and in the East Bay. Indeed you will see it this evening on your ferry ride back to San Francisco. The Square has been awarded city, state and federal landmark status. The Square has shops and restaurants, but what is more pertinent for you at this point is a lovely courtyard where you can sit with one of those huge delicious ice-cream treats.

At about quarter to two hail a taxi and tell the driver to take you to the parking lot adjoining the **Golden Gate Bridge Gift Center**

Buying crabs at Fisherman's Wharf

located at the entrance to the bridge. You will see a statue of Joseph B. Strauss, the man behind the bridge, and right next to him, a cable on display. Continue walking past the statue to your right and you will get some lovely shots of the bridge. Take a quick look at the Center, but then you mustn't tarry too long before beginning your 1.7-mile (2.7-km) walk across

50th Anniversary Golden Gate Bridge Walk

the icon of San Francisco. This suspension bridge was started on 5 January, 1933 and completed on 27 May, 1937.

More than 100,000 tons of steel were used over a period spanning 25,000,000 man hours. Eleven men were killed during the construction. It was the first bridge in the world to experiment with one-way toll collection and is painted a dusky orange. Not golden, like its name implies, but orange. The original plan was to paint the approach pylons on either side of the bridge gold, but no one ever took that seriously. The chief engineer, who thought most bridges were boring because they were gray, had suggested a silvery aluminum color, much like the color chosen for the Bay Bridge.

Irving Morrow, the bridge district's consulting architect, is generally thought to be the man responsible for the final color, a blend of orange and black paint that is unique to the Golden Gate Bridge. But the bridge does look golden when the sun sets behind it and when the day is clear enough for you to see it!

Most people will not think of walking across the bridge so it is very unlikely that you will encounter large groups. This was not so in 1986 when the city celebrated the 50th anniversary of the bridge. 800,000 adventurers crowded the bridge, met half way, found it difficult to turn around or move on and then stood in fright as the bridge swayed.

Ignore the cars that whiz along the asphalt and concentrate on the **Marin Headlands** in front of you, San Francisco behind and the sea on either side. On a warm day you might not need a jacket, but it is generally very windy so the jacket you brought along will really come in handy now. Take your time. You can get some exquisite shots from this vantage point.

Bridgeway Street, Sausalito

As you start walking, look down on the massive brick **Fort Point**. When you pass the second tower of the bridge, you will have officially stepped into **Marin County**. The bridge ends at **Vista Point**, where people can enjoy the sensation of being above water, looking at the sailboats passing by or even waving to the people below who are enjoying the waves.

When you have crossed the bridge, follow **Alexander Avenue**, a narrow, winding road that will lead you to **Sausalito**. Should you not want to walk to Sausalito, have the taxi meet you at Vista Point and then drive you to town. That is an option for those of you who are not big walkers or who get tired quickly. If there is a back-up on the bridge you will walk past an endless line of cars whose occupants will regard you with envy. Don't be surprised if a frustrated driver offers to sell you his car and then, when he sees you walking on, yells, "It's free, take it." Be careful on this narrow street. But if you walk on the left side and don't wander too far onto the tar, it should prove no problem. Soon you will see the bay on your right and houses dotting the hill on your left. Keep walking, past the wooden houses, past the famous **Chart House** (started by Sally Stanford, one-time saloon woman and madam) until you come to the popular part of Sausalito. Here is the wide sidewalk, the sea crashing onto boulders and numerous art galleries, restaurants, a n t i q u e and gift shops lining the street.

This pretty town-on-the-sea is a well-known haunt for tourists and if you keep your ears open you will hear at least ten languages. You deserve a rest, so seat yourself in the **Bridgeway Café,** the first one on your left

24

and order a coffee and pastry, and prepare to people-watch. The time should be about 4 p.m. at the latest, so you have a while before you catch the **Red and White Ferry** at 5.30 p.m.

When you have finished with your tea, continue down the street, buy a kite or a painting, or even a boat. Sailboats are moored just past the large square that will come up on your right. Remember the square which is in front of the **Sausalito Hotel** because that is where you catch the ferry. If you don't want to walk about the town, sit by the sea and look at the boats on the water.

The ferry makes a brief stop at **Tiburon**, which, in spite of its name (Spanish for shark) is another lovely town. Buy a drink on the ferry and, unless you find it too chilly, sit up on top to watch San Francisco get closer and closer. You will pass **Angel Island** (the big island) and **Alcatraz** (the smaller island with the big building) before landing at Fisherman's Wharf. If it is dark you will see the sign for **Ghirardelli Square** grow bigger and bigger.

By now the Wharf is known territory so you should feel like a native as you hail a taxi to take you to **Square One** (190 Pacific Avenue). This is one of the more popular restaurants in San Francisco and serves Californian cuisine at its best. It is a small, discreet place which makes up in food what it lacks in ambience. The decor is stark, but the food is always first rate. Usually listed in restaurant guides under "Mediter-ranean", but I have found the cuisine to be more *nouvelle* Californian. The menus change daily but it doesn't seem to matter what the cook does, it always tastes wonderful.

End your first day by having a drink at the **Top of the Mark**. This is a well-known landmark of San Francisco, situated on Nob Hill, the place Robert Louis Stevenson once called "the hill of palaces". Nearly 20 years after the Mark Hopkins Institute of Art − originally the home of Mark Hopkins − burned in the 1906 fire, the **Hotel Mark Hopkins** rose in its place. The Top of the Mark opened in 1939, the year of the Golden Gate Exposition. Relax, have a drink in this skyroom and look down upon the city as it glows into the night.

49-Mile Drive and Steller Sea Lions

Breakfast at Mama's ($); Coit tower; Filbert Steps to the oldest park in the city; lunch at Cliff House ($); 49-Mile Drive; dinner at Trader Vic's ($$$); comedy at Finocchio's.

What to do before: rent a car, preferably an automatic with excellent brakes (see our "What To Know" section for rental agencies); call Trader Vic's at 776-2232 to make a 7 p.m. dinner reservation. NB: Trader Vic's observes a dress code.

Drivers know San Francisco alternately as the **City of Seven Hills** and as the **City of One Way Streets**. So be a native today and join all the others who drive around this small city looking for parking and streets that allow you to turn left. Besides, you cannot truly belong to San Francisco unless you know how to stop and start on a hill without rolling back, park effectively on a hill and develop a third eye for finding parking spaces.

Bring along change for the parking meters. Meter maids are very vigilant; some cars even carry signs "Meter maids eat their children". Valid licences from Western nations authorize their owners to drive in California without further licensing for one year. Persons from other countries must possess a current international driver's licence.

The following are some facts you need to know when driving in San Francisco: keep a sharp eye out for one-way streets and "Do not turn left" signs. If you park in a residential area, make sure you are not parking on the wrong side during street-cleaning day. Do not, under any circumstances, park at bus stops and fire hydrants. The violation alone may cost up to $100 plus a $150 for towing and storage fees per day.

The curb colors should be strictly adhered to and are decoded as follows: red means no stopping or parking, yellow means a half-hour limit for loading vehicles with commercial plates, yellow and black allow a half-hour limit for trucks with commercial plates, blue indicates a zone for the handicapped, green permits a ten-minute stop and white a five-minute stop, effective during the relevant business hours of operation. Should you be forced to park on a hill, turn the tires toward the street when facing uphill so that they rest against the curb, and towards the curb when facing downhill, in order to use the curb as a block against rolling forwards.

This is for your information only. The itinerary for today is planned so that you will have no trouble at all finding parking spaces. If for some reason or other you have to park on a hill and you still feel unsure despite my instructions, look at the other cars and follow accordingly.

Breakfast today is at **Mama's**, a veritable San Franciscan institution. Breakfast here and you can say you have been to San Francisco. Mama's is situated at one corner of **Washington Square Park** at 1701 Stockton, and you will find plenty of parking spaces along the side streets.

Washington Square Park is one of three parks that were reserved as such in the city plan of 1847, though its present look is courtesy of a 1955 face lift. In its center is a **statue of Benjamin Franklin**, presented to the city in 1879.

The restaurant is located in **North Beach**, a section of town filled with cafés, bookshops, art galleries and music. The area is named after a beach that used to exist on what is Francisco Street today. North Beach burned in 1906, but it was re-built quickly. It is also known as the Italian section because of the Italians who settled here in the early part of this century. The area was put on the map in the 1950s with the arrival of the beatniks. Not much is left of that time except for the **City Lights Bookstore** on Columbus and Broadway, and **Vesuvio's**, a lovely bar.

Mama's is relatively small but at nine in the morning you should be able to get a window seat. You will have a lovely view of the park though you will not be able to see the **Church of St Peter and St Paul** that is just further up from Mama's on the same side of the street. Cecil B. DeMille filmed part of *The Ten Commandments* at this church. The church's inscription is the opening of the first canto of Dante's *Paradiso* and it remains the spiritual

Coit Tower

home of San Francisco's Italian-Americans. You can also watch the cook whip up your breakfast behind the counter.

After breakfast, follow the signs to **Coit Tower** on Telegraph Hill. The road winds up till you come to a parking lot, and unless this is a weekend, you should have no trouble getting a space. Step out of the car and you will realize that you don't *have* to take the elevator to the top of Coit Tower in order to get a wonderful view of the city and the bay. Even the most jaded of San Franciscans will testify to that. If you prefer your scenery up close, just put money in the telescope.

Coit Tower mural

All around the parking lot runs a sidewalk that is filled with vendors selling souvenirs. You can buy sweat shirts, T-shirts, caps, shades, magnets and paintings. This is a popular place for school children so do not be surprised if you come on a morning when third-graders are having a drawing lesson.

Climb the steps to the tower and go to the bulletin board that will tell you all about the tower and the woman who made it possible. The walls are covered with **murals** depicting scenes of manual labor. The murals were sponsored during the 1930s, and were done in six months by 25 master artists and 19 assistants. The famous Mexican artist Diego Rivera influenced many of those who painted the murals.

Indoors you will find a machine which yields a commemorative penny for 50 cents and the tower also has a **gift shop** that sells everything from heart-shaped erasers stamped "San Francisco" to lovely post cards.

Ride the elevator for the view. Even if it is a foggy day you will still be delighted by it. If you happen to go during **Fleet week**, you will see huge ships anchored in the bay.

Once outside the tower, turn right and look for the sign that reads Greenwich. Walk down the slope on your right until you reach the sign for the **Filbert Steps.**

Follow the sign down to the wooden steps and you will see wonderful foliage on either side. Numerous cats make this place their haunt so it is entirely possible that you might have to share the steps with a feline friend. When you reach **Montgomery Street** look to your left. Behind a fire hydrant is a mural depicting a dog with these words: "No dogs/ Teacup poodles ok". The **Filbert Steps** epitomize the essence of San Francisco. Here is a colorful gateway of flowers and greenery so close to – and yet so far from – the Embarcadero and the bustle of business life. It reminds you once again that you are in a city of color; even the houses are painted in pastels.

Traipse up the stairs when you are done with them and get ready to do the **49-Mile Scenic Drive,** which was marked out in 1939, the year of the Golden Gate Exposition. At that time it began and ended on Treasure Island and was a quick way of getting visitors familiarized with the city. It was so popular that the drive has been maintained by the Department of Public Works ever since. Though tell most San Franciscans about the 49-Mile Drive and they will probably say, "Where?" Ask about the seagull sign that guides the driver along the way and they will doubtless say, "What?" But don't let that faze you. Driving is a wonderful way of getting to know the city as vistas change from green trees to blue sea to windmills.

But I suggest you don't drive the whole route, which, incidentally, has been modified over the years. In 1969 the drive was changed to include Japantown. If you follow my guideline, you will begin at **Coit Tower** and end at **Mission Dolores**, bypassing Civic Center, Chinatown, Nob Hill and the Financial District. But with the exception of the Financial District, you will be visiting the other areas later.

So leave Coit Tower and go down **Lombard Street**. Before you follow the seagull and turn right on **Mason Street**, you have the option of continuing on Lombard to the zig-zag part of the street. Doubtless you have already seen postcards featuring this crooked street which loops down the hill between gardens filled with beautiful flowers. I've left it open as an option just in case you don't feel comfortable driving down it. Or conversely, you can drive up, look down and then return to the 49-Mile (79-km) Drive venue. (Other Street information: The oldest street is Grant Avenue; the longest street: Mission Street; the widest street: Van Ness Avenue; the narrowest street: De Forest Way; and the steepest street: Filbert Street, between Leavenworth and Hyde streets.)

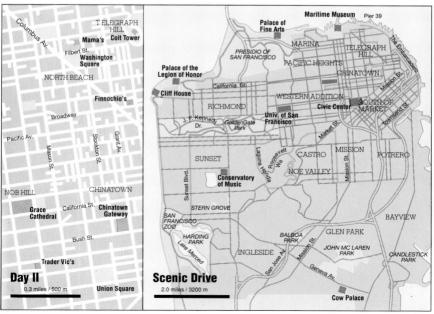

Back on Mason you will turn into **Jefferson Street** and the Fisherman's Wharf. You are bound to do a certain amount of backtracking in your four days because San Francisco is a small city.

As you approach **Hyde Street**, don't forget to look at the **Aquatic Park**, the **Hyde Street Pier** and the **Maritime Museum**. The museum and the park were the product of a project in 1939 to create a place for the city people to swim and have fun in a "healthy" way. The museum used to be a casino and had shower facilities for bathers. The casino was not a business success and the building was turned into a museum in 1950. Notice the

Aquatic Park

beautiful houses – with large bay windows and pretty colors – on your left as you drive past the **Marina Green.** The Marina was the area most affected by the fire that broke out after the 1989 earthquake. Even though the area is landfill and could possibly liquify during another earthquake, nobody is selling. It used to be a prized neighborhood and apparently the calamity has not convinced people otherwise.

Watch out for the **seagull sign** to turn left on **Scott Street** or you will likely end up on the Golden Gate Bridge. The **Palace of Fine Arts** is an old San Francisco landmark though it was only built in 1915 for the Panama-Pacific International Exposition. But San Francisco is a pretty young city and anything close to the turn of the century qualifies as old. Designed by Bernard Maybeck, one of the Bay Area's foremost architects, it houses the **Exploratorium**, an internationally acclaimed **museum of science, art and human perception** featuring about 650 exhibits that can be manipulated or activated by push-buttons.

The Palace of Fine Arts

The drive makes a loop and then moves into the **Presidio**, providing an abrupt, albeit beautiful, shift of scenery and ambience. The Presidio was occupied by a Spanish garrison in 1776 and today the 1,500 acres (600 hectares) is the headquarters of the Sixth Army. But driving through this verdant, peaceful area it is hard to believe that an army resides here. If the tall trees and the tranquility appeal to you, take a brief leave of

The Cliff House Restaurant

absence from the 49-Mile Drive and explore it on your own.

A little further you will drive past the **California Palace of the Legion of Honor**, a replica of the one in Paris. It is very grand and stands proudly on its vantage point, commanding respect. The museum (check before you go; it may be closed for renovations) contains masterpieces of **European art** from medieval times to the 20th century, including works by Rodin, Rembrandt, El Greco, Titian, Corot, Fragonard, Manet, Cezanne, Renoir and Goya.

Then you drive towards the ocean and come to **Point Lobos,** which houses the **Cliff House,** the **Sutro Baths** and **Seal Rock.** Stop for lunch and though I can't enthuse about the cuisine, Cliff House does provide a wonderful view. This is the fifth version of the Cliff House built on the same site since the mid-19th century. Don't forget to wander into the **Phineas T. Barnacle Room**, the only bar in the world whose mirrors are acid-etched with photographs taken by Ansel Adams. The famous photographer did the acid-etching himself. Keep in mind for future reference that the Cliff House is a perfect place in which to have a drink and watch the sunset.

Although you cannot do that yet in the early afternoon, you can watch the seals, walk down to the baths, and if you are really in the mood, climb the steps opposite the Cliff House to **Sutro Park**. Adolph Sutro's baths of 1896 are now ruins though once they held 10,000 people. The **Seal Rocks** are a favorite spot for Steller sea lions and their melancholy loud barking competes with the fog horns. Congress deeded these rocks to the city in 1887, from which time the sea lions have been under the protection of the Recreation and Park Commission. They go away to breed in June but otherwise are a common sight. The **Musee Mecanique** in the Cliff House has a fascinating show tracing the development of arcade games right up to Space Invaders. You can even walk along the beach at the base of the cliffs, but put on something warm and do not, under any circumstances swim, because there are strong currents here.

Just before you turned into the Cliff House, you will have seen some cliffs on your right. Hikers should make a note of this; the cliffs are part of the **Golden Gate Recreational Area** and are dissected with paths that lead to wonderful vistas.

For a while now you will drive with the ocean to your right and fields to your left. If you concentrate too much on the sea, you will

miss the two windmills. The first, the **Dutch Windmill**, stands without its blades and was built in 1903. The second, called **Murphy Windmill**, was built in 1905 and has blades. Both are part of the Golden Gate Park which you will drive through later.

You may stop at **Ocean Beach**, but don't tarry, for you are coming up to one of the great events of the drive: **Golden Gate Park**.

Murphy Windmill

I will not even try describing the park for you; I will just tell you that every time I drive through it, it takes my breath away. No matter what the season or the occasion for going there, I leave feeling refreshed and peaceful. No wonder, then, that it is the haunt for joggers, families and lovers.

The park itself is a miracle, for who would have dreamed that sand could yield such beauty? In the 1860s this three-mile (five-km) long, half-mile (800-meter) wide tract of land was sheer sand. In 1871, William Hammond Hall was commissioned to begin the long process of restoration. Hall and the city did not work well together, but fortunately his successor, Scotsman John McLaren, did. "Uncle" John took up the cause of the park and continued doing so till his death at age 96 in 1943. McLaren was a perfectionist who, legend has it, stopped at nothing to get his way. His memory lives on in the

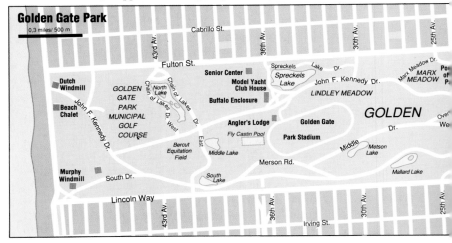

perfection of the park. Since the park is so lovely, you should make the most of it by following your eyes rather than the seagull.

Roll down the windows of the car to let in the smell of the greenery, and get your camera ready. Prepare for rapid changes of scenery, from wide lakes to blooming flowers, tall trees, waterfalls and buffalos.

You must stop at the **Conservatory of Flowers,** the **Rhododendron Dell** if it's May, and the **Strybing Arboretum.** The Conservatory, a white Victorian greenhouse, is the oldest building in the park. It was ordered to be designed in 1875 from Dublin by millionaire James Lick for his house in San Jose. The Dell is a four-acre (1.6-hectare) memorial to McLaren who is

The Conservatory of Flowers

represented by a statue – he, who fought against having any statues in the park! But when the flowers are in bloom, you will understand why this spot was chosen to honor the man who made the park what it is today.

The **Arboretum** contains over three thousand species of plants. Look out for the many ducks and swans that roam around this 60-acre (24-hectare) wonderland.

Stop for tea at the **Japanese Tea Garden** just west of **de Young Museum.** The garden itself is old, having been developed for the 1894 fair by George Turner Marsh, who opened the first oriental art store in America. The Hagiwara family operated a tea garden in these premises from 1907 to 1942, and it was here in 1909 that the world's first fortune cookies were introduced. So although fortune cookies are associated with Chinese restaurants – Chinatown quickly capitalized on this bit of good luck which kept the customers happy and coming – they are a Japanese invention. During the Japanese

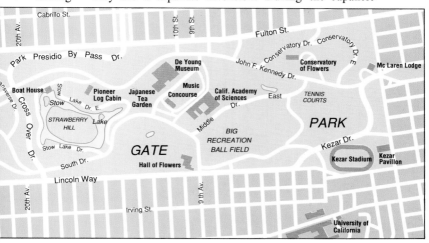

incarceration in World War II, the Hagiwaras were sent to camp in Utah and the city renamed the family business the **Oriental Tea Garden**. This five-acre (two-hectare) garden was given its original name in 1952 and today draws thousands of people to its beautiful setting.

View from Twin Peaks

In this little bit of Japan, tea is served by waitresses dressed in kimonos and the garden is replete with arched bridges, bonsai, large fish and azaleas that bloom in spring. There is a **gift shop** at the top of the rise where you can buy beautiful chopsticks, small purses as well as other trinkets.

But beyond these suggestions, feel free to explore the park and stop whenever you like. A warning: don't get side-tracked by the **Shakespeare garden**. Only flowers that are mentioned throughout Shakespeare's plays are on display.

You won't have time to visit the museum but save it for later. **Stow Lake** is a safe place for boating, unlike the chimerical bay. There is an island in the center of the lake which is easily accessible to walkers and which surprises with its view.

The next highlight on this drive is the winding road up to **Twin Peaks** and the magnificent view afforded from that height. Watch for the seagull which points left from Woodside Avenue to Twin Peaks Boulevard; it's easy to miss. Once on Twin Peaks, park the car and get out to enjoy the panorama. A directory will help you locate places. This is a very popular spot at night and if you really like it, you might want to return sometime during your stay for the night air and the magical view of a city dotted with lights.

From Twin Peaks you drive straight through a rather bland part of the city till you come to **Mission Dolores**, one of the 21 California missions. Today it stands on a wide road separated into two by an island of grass. The mission was completed in 1791 and is the oldest intact building in San Francisco. Its official name is the Mission San Francisco de Asis though it is commonly known as Mission Dolores.

Mission Dolores

It doesn't take long to the see the mission, so park the car on the street and go on inside. The ceilings are repainted, but remain spectacular, depicting original Indian designs done with vegetable dyes. The statues as well as the altar came from Mexico and were added in the early 1800s.

The Museum was established in 1976, the bicentennial year of Mission Dolores, and contains the baptismal register dating from 1776. Many people are buried in the cemetery, including Don Luis Antonia Arguello, the first governor of Alta California under Mexican rule.

This is where I leave off guiding you through this scenic drive. There will be plenty to occupy you till the evening. Dinner is at **Trader Vic's**, popular long before Queen Elizabeth graced the restaurant with her royal presence. The restaurant is tucked away at 20 Cosmo Place, you will be pleased and surprised to find that Trader Vic's is not merely a restaurant, it is

a sort of **museum**. It is an experience that involves more than just eating. Everyone in the Bay Area tries to go there at least once. Even poor college students like to go to Trader Vic's if only to order one of their famous rum drinks. Victor J. Bergeron was a collector, and you will find artifacts from the islands he loved all over the walls and ceilings. Those of you who are interested can spend time in the lobby and even buy his book, *Trader Vic's Helluva Man's Cookbook*.

The cuisine is oriental/continental and the service is impeccable. Try strange-sounding *bongo bongo* soup and Pake crab; exotic names meant to remind you of Polynesia. Don't forget to order a drink. They have very creative ways of serving them so look forward to getting something fun.

Finocchio's is located at 506 Broadway, one of the main streets in Frisco's famed Barbary Coast. The bawdy traditions of the Gold Rush town were carried on quite profitably along Broadway until a few years ago when this part of North Beach went into a period of decay. Most of the old topless strip joints are now closed and many of the good restaurants and legitimate nightclubs have migrated to other parts of town – many to the SoMa (South of Market) area. If you're looking for the remnants of the old "sporting life" you'll find them downtown in the Tenderloin District, most especially near Geary and Polk and around the Hilton Hotel. But take care. The Tenderloin is dark and dangerous.

Skip the above titillation and proceed to your entertainment for tonight. For 50 years Finocchio's has provided fabulous female impersonators in four lavish revues starting every night at 8.30 p.m. The men are so good it is difficult to believe they are not women. The show represents an aspect of San Francisco that is very well known.

Finocchio's is closed on Monday and Tuesday. So if you are unlucky, go to **The Improv**. It's located at 401 Mason Street, which is within walking distance from Trader Vic's. The Improv draws the best stand-up comics in the business and is a very comfortable club.

Day 3

Chinese Dim Sum and Japanese Massage

Chinatown; dim sum at Tung Fong ($); Shiatsu massage at Kabuki Hot Springs; dinner at the Hayes Street Grill (closed Sunday) ($$), concert, drinks at Act IV; or dinner at China Moon Café ($$), theater; drinks at Regina's.

What to do before: call 922-6000 to make a 2 p.m. appointment for a massage at Kabuki Hot Springs; call the Hayes Street Grill at 863-5545 or the China Moon Café at 775-4789 to make a 6 p.m. dinner reservation; call **Bass** (510-762-2277) for tickets to either the concert or theater.

Today you will discover why Duke Ellington once said, "San Francisco is one of the great cultural plateaus of the world". You will have two different cultural experiences: one you enjoy via a ticket and acquire while sitting in a hall; the other from mixing with vibrant San Franciscans who prove that variety is the vital ingredient for growth.

Get up leisurely – you deserve it – and don't have anything more than a coffee. Just like Day One, put on a sturdy pair of walking shoes, though today's walk will be less brisk and more stop-and-go. At about 10 a.m. take a taxi to **Chinatown**.

Get off at **Chinatown Gateway**, the great dragon-crested gate at Bush and Grant. Your morning in Chinatown, like that first day at Fisherman's Wharf, is yours to do with as you wish.

Many Chinese live above the shops and restaurants like their forefathers did. Chinatown today is a central part of the San Francisco experience, yet in the last century and well into this one, the Chinese were not welcome in the city.

The first Chinese were miners who came to *gum san,* or Gold Mountain, in the middle of the 19th century. They suffered poor working conditions, low pay, anti-miscegenation laws and laws limiting immigration. They were incarcerated on Angel Island and their women were sold into prostitution. San Francisco even implemented its own laws. There was a queue tax, a pole law prohibiting the use of car-

Grant Avenue, Chinatown

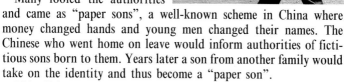

rying baskets on poles, cigar taxes, shoes taxes and laundry taxes. Once the need for laborers was over, the Chinese were no longer needed. But they refused to leave, giving rise to the infamous "Chinese problem".

Many fooled the authorities and came as "paper sons", a well-known scheme in China where money changed hands and young men changed their names. The Chinese who went home on leave would inform authorities of fictitious sons born to them. Years later a son from another family would take on the identity and thus become a "paper son".

This Chinese problem was dealt with on Angel Island, where immigrants were held and questioned in minute detail. "How many steps are there in your house?" "Did your family have a dog in 1899?" The 1906 calamity benefitted the Chinese. All the citizenship papers were burned in the fire that ensued after the earthquake, and so every Chinaman was re-born an American.

Today, the Chinese, along with other Asian-Americans, are widely-respected. Some of them, like Mr. Tom Hsieh, have achieved political prominence in San Francisco.

When you get hungry, go to **Tung Fong** at 808 Pacific Avenue for dim sum. Be there before noon to avoid the lunch rush, though typically dim sum begins at 11 a.m. This is quite definitely the thing to do while in Chinatown. You don't have to say a word. Just sit down at a table, waiters will bring trays of food. Point to the ones you want to eat. Dim sum means "a little heart" and the food reflects that sentiment. Dumplings, small bite-size pieces of various ingredients, make for fun eating. Order some Chinese tea to wash it down with. At the end of the meal, the plates you have on your table are counted in order to tabulate the bill.

After lunch you can look for gifts or take pictures. At about a quarter to two, take a taxi to Geary Boulevard to the **Kabuki Hot Springs** (1750 Geary Boulevard) for the treat of your life. Whether you had arranged for a half-hour massage or an hour's massage, the procedure is the same. First they enclose you (head out) in a steam cabinet for 15 minutes or so. Next your back is dry scrubbed with natural sponge. Then you soak your muscles in a hot bath. After 15 minutes of relaxation comes the best part: the massage.

This should put you in a good mood for the evening's entertainment deep in the cultural heart of San Francisco. There is opera, symphony, ballet and theater. The program varies widely, from Pavarotti to Russian dancing.

If you have tickets for either the opera, the symphony or the ballet, take your place with the other cultureophiles at the **Hayes Street Bar & Grill** (324 Hayes Street). This

is a very popular pre-concert restaurant whose co-owner, Patricia Unterman, is one of the food critics for the *San Francisco Chronicle*. So be assured of sympathetic company, good food, and service that understands your need to be in another seat by 8 p.m. Take a leisurely stroll to the concert venue, and don't forget to appreciate the grand buildings that make this part of San Francisco like Vienna, all gilt and grandeur. **Davies Symphony Hall** is quite a new building while the **Opera House** is old San Francisco.

After the concert, race – and I mean race – over to **Act IV** at 333 Fulton Street for a drink. This is where you will find everyone who is anyone. For today you have demonstrated that you can definitely be counted as a San Franciscan. In three days you have proven that you can drive with the best of them, you know where to find the best views and you can even race the old-timers out of a seat.

If you have decided on the theater, the venue for dinner will be different. Take a taxi to **China Moon Café** on 639 Post Street between Jones and Taylor. Chef-cum-owner Barbara Tropp uses fresh ingredients to create authentic Chinese dishes. Those of you who are interested in Chinese cooking can buy her book, *The Modern Art of Chinese Cooking*. The theaters are within walking distance from the restaurant, so you will have plenty of time to enjoy the food. Be sure to get there before the curtain rises, otherwise you might have to sit out the first act.

After the play, depart with the others to **Regina's** (490 Geary St.) for a drink and if you find you are still hungry, you can order a decadent New Orleans dessert that is part doughnut, part ice cream, and smothered with praline sauce.

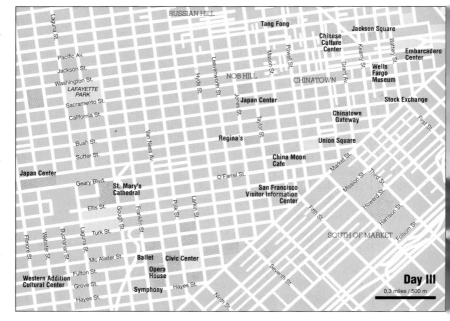

Day 4

Expensive Shopping and Ferry to Alcatraz

Breakfast at Sear's (open Wed to Sunday) ($); shopping at Union Square; lunch at Macy's ($$); tour of Alcatraz; dinner at Julius' Castle ($$$).

What to do before: call Bass at 510-762-2277 for tickets to Alcatraz. Tickets can prove to be a real problem during the summer months so you might have to get up early and stand in line at the **Alcatraz Ticket Booth** at Pier 41, Fisherman's Wharf. You can ask for a tour in Japanese, German, French or Spanish. Make dinner reservations at Julius' Castle, 362-3042.

Today is the day for extremes. You will boomerang from the 1950s to the 1990s, from the comfort of deep pile carpeting to the confines of a small cell, from the expensive and elite San Francisco to wind-whipping spray in your face. So wear something nice but remember to bring along something warm as well.

Neiman Marcus window display

Your day will begin in another time, courtesy of **Sear's Fine Food** restaurant at 439 Powell Street. Get there before 9 a.m. to beat the long lines. This old-time eatery has a devoted following, both foreign and local. But if there is a line, do not despair. Mr. Lee, the owner, promises that you won't have to wait more than ten minutes. Once inside, you will be treated to dining 1950s style – with 1990s prices, however. The waitresses wear red and white uniforms and bobby socks. The tables have lace tablecloths covered with clear plastic. Sear's is famous – and justly so – for its Swedish pancakes, all 18 varieties of them.

Union Square is the shopping haven of San Francisco, with Sear's at its heart; and around it are the famous boutiques of Saks Fifth Avenue, Burberry's of London, Macy's, I. Magnin and Neiman Marcus, Gucci, Tiffany, Jaeger, Brooks Brothers, Ralph Lauren, Celine, Pierre Deux, Laura Ashley and Cartier. **FAO Schwartz** has delightful pet animals. If you do not want to poke around too many stores, just go to **Macy's**. Cross the street for the menswear department and there is a café downstairs for refreshments.

FAO Schwartz

The other stores have eating places as well; **I. Magnin** has Narsai's downstairs while **Nordstrom** even has a champagne bar. Rest your weary feet and fill your stomach at either of these places for lunch.

Alcatraz emblem

Nordstrom will drive you (and your packages) to your hotel if you want to skip lunch outside and eat something in your room before taking the Alcatraz tour. For more shopping see the section headed "Shopping". After lunch, drop your parcels at your hotel, take the cable car to Fisherman's Wharf, and walk to **Pier 41**. Clamber onto the Red & White Ferry that will take you to prison.

Known familiarly as "the rock", the 22 ½ - acre (9-hectare) **Isla de Alcatraces** (Spanish for pelican) was named in August 1775 by Lt. Juan Manuel de Ayola, commander of the survey vessel *San Carlos*, the first known ship to enter the San Francisco Bay. The Alcatraz lighthouse, built in 1854, was the first one in the bay. In 1859 the island was occupied by troops and was the province of the army till

Alcatraz Island

1 January 1934, when it became a Federal penitentiary. It served as the supermaximum security prison for the likes of Al Capone, Mickey Cohen, Robert Stroud, and Joseph "Dutch" Critzer. Indeed it is these inmates who made the island famous. Today Alcatraz stands unoccupied, a symbol of an outmoded era in penology. Although San Francisco lay within swimming reach, the bay was treacherous. Only two prisoners managed to escape and since they were never heard of again, authorities believed they perished in the waters.

In 1969 Sioux Indians claimed the island, but were removed in 1971. The island is now part of the 24,000-acre (10,000-hectare) $119-million park-plan called the Golden Gate National Recreation area, approved by President Nixon in 1972.

Today, Alcatraz is a little like Disneyland. You take a fun ferry ride over, visit the prison and then come back to land. The tour includes a historical slide show, an award-winning video tour, as well as a self-guided tour by National Park Service

Alcatraz guard house

Beach St.

Buena Vista North Point St.

Bay St.

Columbus Av. Franciscio St.

Leavenworth St. Chestnut St.

Hyde St.

TELEGRAPH HILL

Stockton St.

Grant Av.

Sansome St.

Lombard St. Coit Tower

Greenwich St. Julius' Castle

Filbert St.

Union St. NORTH BEACH

Green St. RUSSIAN HILL

Taylor St.

Vellejo St. Broadway

Jackson Square

Powell St.

Larkin St. Pacific Av. Chinese Culture Center

Jackson St.

Washington St. NOB HILL Clay St. Wells Fargo Museum

Sacramento St.

CHINATOWN

Grace Cathedral California St. Chinatown Gateway

Kearny St.

Mason St.

Jones St.

Pine St. Crocker Galleria

Bush St. Suffer St.

Day IV Sear's

0.3 miles / 500 m Post St. Union Square

Geary St.

Jil's

guides. You can even be locked up in a cell – but don't worry, you will be let out again, as long as you have not committed any serious crime!

The entire trip will take two hours and should leave you a trifle chilly. So warm your body and your spirits at **Buena Vista**, 2765 Hyde Street. Irish coffee is said to have been concocted here and you simply cannot leave San Francisco without drinking some. It is a wonderful location for you can watch the cable cars turn around and look beyond to the bay and its islands. There should be no crowd at this time of day, but it *is* a very popular place. So if there are lots of people, make sure you are seated and served.

For tonight, your last night in San Francisco, you deserve a room with a view. So take a taxi to **Julius' Castle** (1541 Montgomery Street) where the bay and the city are spread out like a carpet at your feet. You will dine in romance on the finest contemporary European cuisine in a turreted castle.

Pick & Choose

The following itineraries are not as detailed as those of Days 1 -
4. This is because if you have done those routes, you will be quite
familiar with San Francisco by now. All you need are pointers that
will allow you to plan your day according to your interests. By all
means stray from the itineraries if you wish to do so.

A.M. Itineraries

1. Grand and historic San Francisco

**Walk around Nob Hill; cable car to Embarcadero; BART to
Berkeley; lunch at Cafe Pastoral ($$).**

This is the perfect itinerary for
those who want a glimpse of the
the grandeur and pomp of old San
Francisco during the gold-gather-
ing days of the 19th century.
Today the buildings on Nob Hill
survive as proof of that decadent
time of riches. **Nob Hill**, Robert
Louis Stevenson once observed,
was the place "millionaires were
gathered together vying with each
other in display."

Your walk will be bound by the
following streets: Powell, Leaven-
worth, Pine and Clay. I shall dis-
cuss a few particularly noteworthy
and historic buildings. Go ahead,
explore further. No matter where
you go, you will be enchanted
with the architecture and the view.

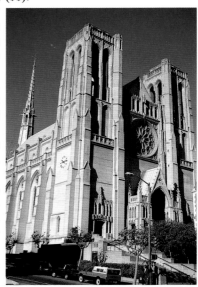
Grace Cathedral

The **Stanford Court Hotel** at 905 California Street was built in
1911 on the site of Leland Stanford's mansion. Stanford was one of

the Big Four of the Central Pacific Railroad, and he, along with the other three, Crocker, Huntington and Hopkins, built grand houses on this hill. Indeed the word "Nob" is thought by some to be a corruption of the Hindi "Nawab", which the British borrowed as a word to describe the rich. Others however, posit that Nob is merely a version of "knob", meaning a rounded hill. Stanford Court is listed as one of San Francisco's best hotels.

If you continue up California Street, you will come to the **Mark Hopkins Inter-Continental Hotel**. It rises on the site of Mark Hopkins's home, which, like the Stanford's, did not survive the fire of 1906. The hotel was designed by Weeks and Day in 1925 and is a getaway for the rich. Walk in and be dazzled.

The only pre-1906 mansion is at 1000 California Street, once the home of James Flood, who made his fortune from silver. Today it is the **Pacific-Union Club**, the city's most prestigious men's club.

Mark Hopkins Inter-Continental Hotel

The **Fairmont Hotel** is well-known to those who saw the popular TV show *Hotel*. It is equally well-known to San Franciscans. The old-timers remember it as the building which once dominated the skyline of the city. The younger generation went to the Venetian Room to be pampered and delighted.

The land was owned by another wealthy man, James G. Fair. His daughter decided to build the most lavish hotel in San Francisco. It was completed just before the disaster of 1906, which left the exterior standing but ruined the sumptuous furnishings. Not to be daunted and in true San Franciscan temperament, the hotel was opened one year – to the day – after the fire. Don't miss out on riding the **glass-walled elevator** which rises slowly while all around you unfolds the breathtaking panorama of the city.

Fairmont Hotel

Every wall has a story to tell. So does **Huntington Park**, given to the city in 1915 by the widow of the railway magnate and once the site of a mansion belonging to David Colton, the chief lawyer for the railroad. The Big Four sued him posthumously on the claim that he had embezzled railroad money. During the sensational trial, Mrs Colton tainted Huntington's reputation by exhibiting letters he had written her husband detailing how the railroad baron had "bought" politicians in Washington. Mrs. Colton sold the mansion in 1880 and 12 years later it was purchased by none other than Huntington.

Today, the green park is a far cry from scandal and slander and remains one of the nicest in San Francisco. It has a **replica of the Tartarughe Fountain** copied from the Piazza Mattei in Rome. The ornate structure with the red tiled roof is a public toilet.

Grace Cathedral is the pride and joy of the city, both for those who attend service in this hallowed haven and also for those who are not religious. Inspired by Notre Dame, the structure definitely reminds one of the Gothic style. George Bodley drew the initial plans which Lewis Hobart then completed. Take a look at the Washington elm near the steps. The tree comes from Cambridge, the very one under which George Washington accepted command of the American troops. Remember to check the Pink Pages of the Sunday newspaper for events happening at the cathedral. Sometimes it serves as a stage for plays, such as T. S. Eliot's *Murder in the Cathedral*.

When you are through with Nob Hill, walk down to California and Van Ness to catch the

Grace Cathedral windows

cable car, though you can get on at any of the stops en route. Take it all the way to the end and then look for the **BART** sign and steps leading underground to the Embarcadero Station. This is the superfast subway system that links the city to Richmond, Concord and Fremont in the East Bay. You want the Richmond line, which will take you to Berkeley. The fare should be $1.80, the ticket is available from the unmanned dispenser on the wall near the turnstile. This is an exciting half-hour ride because the train goes under the bay before coming out into the light at Oakland West. Get off at Berkeley (don't get confused by North Berkeley, which is the next station) and take the Constitution Plaza exit. That will put you at Shattuck and Center. Walk north towards University Avenue (Waldenbooks is on your left and you should walk away from it) and turn right. It is a very busy street which ends where the Berkeley Campus begins.

But before that, on your right you will see **Cafe Pastoral** (2160 University Avenue). A very popular spot for lunch, the restaurant offers French cuisine with an oriental twist. The food is delicious and

the presentation excellent. It is rumored that the paintings on the wall are by the owner's wife. But don't let her gloomy pictures get to you, have a good lunch.

BART – rapid transit

2. Hiking in historic Muir Woods

A glimpse of what California must have looked like centuries ago; bring along a picnic lunch to eat on the fallen trunk of a grand old tree, one with secrets we shall never know.

The redwoods here evolved about 150 million years ago and became common in this part of the world from 30 to 10 million years ago. That alone is impressive but wait till you see them in their setting. Get a map, decide how long you want to hike, and go for it. **Muir Woods** provides a good picture of the California of yore.

Take **Highway 101** across the Golden Gate Bridge and go west on Highway 1 at the **Stinson Beach exit**. About three miles (five km) later, turn right on Panoramic Highway and after one mile (1.6 km) turn left on Muir Woods Road and keep going till you come to the parking lot which gives access to the woods that are indeed "lovely, dark and deep."

All of us who enjoy the woods today are indebted to William Kent, who bought the first 300 acres (120 hectares) of this canyon in 1905. In 1908 President Theodore Roosevelt made it a national monument and named it after John Muir, founder of the Sierra Club. Kent deeded more land and today the 550-acre (222-hectare) park is administered by the GGNRA (Golden Gate National Recreation Area). It is open from eight in the morning to sunset and is almost always crowded.

It is a wonderful way to spend the morning. If you find that there are a bit too many people about, just keep walking. The further you go, the less likely are you to find them.

Redwoods in the Muir Woods

Enjoy the sporting activities in Golden Gate Park, and mingle with the natives enjoying the fresh air.

The Golden Gate Park is a city in itself and thus warrants many visits. A friend of mine who runs there daily says he is a little fed up because he knows every bump in the path and every tree along the way. Suggest he run elsewhere and he says, "What, are you crazy?"

This park, an embodiment of how San Francisco feels about nature, is very different from parks around the world simply because it is used and enjoyed so much more. In part, of course, we have the sunny weather to thank. Some San Franciscans walk their dogs here every morning and evening; others jog here after a hard day at work; some come by to enjoy the flowers; the museum buffs stop off at **de Young**; yoga fans think nothing of finding a quiet green spot for their *asanas* (poses); while others, like you, go boating in **Stow Lake**.

Boating here is completely safe compared to on the waters of the Bay. If you are not up to a rowboat, rent a pedal boat or an electric motorboat. The **boathouse** is on the north side where you can arrange for the rental of boats and for refreshments.

This man-made lake is named after the park commissioner who persuaded railroad magnate Huntington to construct it. The lake was one of the more heavily used areas of the park in the last century. At that time the island, called Strawberry Hill, had an observation tower which was later destroyed in the 1906 quake. You can still see bits of the pink foundation. **Strawberry Hill** is likewise a man-made hill and you might check to see if wild strawberries still grow on it. You will enjoy a panoramic view of San Francisco from its summit.

When you are hungry, drive over to **Marnee Thai** ($) at 2225 Irving, between 23rd and 24th avenues. This is a busy part of town, especially during lunch hour. So do what any San Franciscan would: keep an eye out for a parking space and as soon as you see one available, take it.

Marnee Thai is a good Thai restaurant which offers lunch specials. If you are in a hurry, tell your waitress and she will do her best to serve you quickly. The decor is fairly commonplace. The food is less spicy than typical Thai food so as to accommodate foreign palates. So if you don't mind chilies, tell your waitress and order accordingly.

P.M. Itineraries

1. House Browse in Pacific Heights

Walk down quiet streets lined with trees; the neighborhood offers a counterpoint to the hustle and bustle of busy San Francisco.

If you enjoy architecture and want to see how one special segment of San Francisco lives, an afternoon spent in Pacific Heights is the perfect choice. Nob Hill is the last vestige of the very very rich, even though many of the mansions no longer house single families.

Pacific Heights covers the area between Van Ness Avenue, California Street, Presidio Avenue and Union Street. When you visit this area, please respect the residents' privacy. Further west from Pacific Heights is **Presidio Heights**, enclosed by Presidio Avenue, Arguello Boulevard, Clay Street and Pacific Avenue. Go look at the house on the corner of Washington and Maple streets. It's a copy of the Petit Trianon in Versailles.

Style on Pacific Avenue

I shall discuss a few houses below, but do venture beyond and explore as fancy takes you; if you see a "House Open" sign, do go in even if you are not in the market to buy. It will be a good way of getting in without offending anyone.

The **Haas-Lilienthal House** is at 2007 Franklin Street at Jackson Street. William Haas, a grocer of Bavarian extract, built it in 1886. At that time it was one of many such houses in this area. But today it is the lone survivor – the quake and fire of 1906 left it unscathed – and is essentially a "house museum". It contains the offices of the Foundation for San Francisco's Architectural Heritage, a non-profit organisation dedicated to the preservation of buildings and areas important to the city from an architectural and historic standpoint. This fully furnished Victorian House is open to the public on Wednesday, noon - 4 p.m. and Sunday, 11 a.m. - 4.30 p.m.

The Haas-Lilienthal House

Another mansion that welcomes visitors is **Octagon House** at 2645 Gough Street at Union Street. Built in 1861 and bought by the National Society of Colonial Dames of America in 1952, the society supervised the restoration, and furnished it with Colonial and Federal period antique pieces. It is open from noon - 3 p.m. on the second and fourth Thursday and the second Sunday of the month.

Spreckels Mansion is at 2080 Washington Street

47

at Octavia Street, constructed in 1913 on a site that had been home to seven or eight houses. George Applegarth, who designed the house, was the architect for the California Palace of the Legion of Honor. Notice the French influence in both; the museum reflects a French building and the Spreckels Mansion is pure French Baroque.

The **Whittier Mansion** at 2090 Jackson Street is a good example of the brick and stone houses found in Pacific Heights. As the ferocious 1906 fire testified, most San Franciscans then had houses made of wood. The California Historical Society bought the mansion in 1952, and refurnished the house with 19th-century pieces and California paintings. Edward R. Swain, the architect, also designed the McLaren Lodge in Golden Gate Park.

Two other houses worthy of mention are the **James Leary Flood Mansion**, now the Hamlin School, at 2120 Broadway and the **Convent of the Sacred Heart,** at 2222 Broadway Street. Though the former looks like it is built of stone, the material used is wood. The workmanship of the latter is detailed Renaissance.

2. The Mission District

The Mission, one of the oldest parts of the city, is a bustling community of Latinos and counterculture artists and poets.

Start at 24th and York (the 24th St BART station is just six blocks to the east). Stop in at **St. Francis Candies**, right on the corner, for an old-fashioned fountain treat; this ice cream parlor dates back to 1918. Walk to the mini-park across the street to admire the colorful murals; some of these artists are often represented at the **Galeria de la Raza** just a block away (2851 24th St at Bryant; 415-826 8009).

Turn left on Balmy St, three-and-a-half blocks east off 24th St. Virtually every wall space has murals depicting scenes from life in the

Mission District Mural

Mission or in Central American villages. (Precita Eyes Mural Arts Center, 348 Precita Ave, 415-285 2287, offers a guided tour.)

Continue up 24th St, browsing the produce markets, music and clothing stores, bakeries and restaurants – all with a definite Latin American emphasis. **Roosevelt's Tamale Parlor** (2817 24th St) has delicious tamales, and **El Nuevo Frutilandia** (3077 24th St) serves superb Puerto Rican and Cuban dishes.

End your afternoon over a cappuccino at **La Boheme Café** (3318 24th St), just past the intersection of Mission and 24th Sts. Many of the latter-day Bohemians are adorned in black or vintage clothing; their discussions usually range from the French philosophers to the latest art installations. Excellent people-watching.

3. Exploratorium

Take a walk into all the science fiction stories you have ever known; specially suited for children; bring a picnic lunch; (end of Lyon Street, Marina District, closed Monday and Tuesday).

It is very easy to spend a full day here, but because San Francisco is so conducive to the outdoors, I suggest an afternoon visit. The **Exploratorium** is in the **Palace of Fine Arts**, which was built for the Panama-Pacific International Exposition of 1915. I recommend that you eat your picnic lunch on the grounds before going into the museum.

As soon as you enter, all your senses are assaulted. First of all, the room is dark but the exhibits – some 650 of them – are being simultaneously activated by other visitors. What is truly amazing about this museum of science is that every exhibit is meant to be handled. It is somewhat like the Montessori concept of teaching: by touching, seeing and holding. Here you can go from magnets to trick pictures to blowing soap bubbles.

Students from nearby Berkeley often drive into the city just to visit the museum. It is a unique experience that you should not miss.

4. M.H. de Young Memorial Museum

A great favorite as it is in the Golden Gate Park; wide range of displays, including American art from colonial times to the mid-20th century; (open 10 a.m. - 5 p.m., Wednesday to Sunday).

Completed in 1921, de Young is the oldest and largest municipal museum in the west. It is very diversified with an outstanding collection of **American art**, with works by Copley, Sargent, George Caleb Bingham, Winslow Homer and Mary Cassat. There is an outstanding **textile collection** as well as **art from Africa**, Oceania and the two

The de Young Memorial Museum

Americas. The museum has many changing exhibitions, though sometimes tickets are sold out for weeks ahead.

Adjoining the de Young Museum is the **Asian Art Museum** with the **Avery Brundage Collection**. This specially constructed museum was opened in 1966 to house the collection of Avery Brundage. There are over 1,000 objects on display on the main floor, including a 16th-century bell from Tajima Province which, according to tradition, is struck 108 times on New Year's Eve; the second floor features works from Korea, Japan, Tibet and other Asian countries. The museum has the same opening hours as the de Young Museum.

The de Young has a wonderful café where you can sit in the courtyard and forget that a urban area of millions is around you

5. California Academy of Sciences Aquarium, Planetarium and Natural Science Exhibits

Immerse yourself in the astounding exhibits in the Natural History Museum, the Steinhart Aquarium and the Morrison Planetarium; (open daily).

Opposite the de Young Museum and facing the Music Concourse, the Natural History Museum encompasses the **North American Bird and Mammal Hall, Simson African Hall, Hall of Minerals, Lovell White Memorial Hall of Man and Nature, Wattis Hall of Man, Eastwood Hall of Botany** and the **Earth and Space Hall** where visitors can experience an earthquake. For a more humorous time, you can visit the **Far Side of Science Gallery** which features over 160 cartoons by Gary Larson. The **Discovery Room** has hands-on exhibits for children.

Water Monitor Lizard, Steinhart Aquarium

The **Steinhart Aquarium** has some 14,000 aquatic animals and reptiles, including octopi, alligators, turtles, sharks, anemones, seahorses and a two-headed snake. There is a large roundabout tank which brings the ocean and all its species of creatures right to you.

The **Morrison Planetarium** has a specially built 5,000-pound (2,260 kg) star projector. A one-hour sky show takes place daily at 2 p.m. on weekdays. Laserium shows are presented on select evenings.

6. Kite flying at the Marina

Relax in the peaceful field of green that runs between the houses and the sea while kite fanatics around you battle the winds.

San Franciscans think nothing of coming down to the **Marina Green**, sandwich in hand, to watch the kites in the sky and the boats on the sea. Should you get tired of sitting on the grass , you can walk around and find other places of interest.

Sailboats are always moored nearby and it is fun to look at them, or watch a jogger while he runs by, sweat glistening all over his body, or you can walk to the sea and watch the sun set behind the Golden Gate Bridge. Or bring along a book and find a shady spot away from the wind.

Launching 100 kites at the
Marina Green Kite Festival

Nightlife

North Beach rendezvous – Little Italy

What to do before: call 986-1886 to make dinner reservations at the **Fior d' Italia**. ($$)

If you start the evening young enough, it will prove to be a fine mixture of cappuccinos, books and jazz. **North Beach** is a popular hangout for young San Franciscans who come here to take the air that smells of coffee, the 1950s and music. Once their forefathers came here to the beach, but now asphalt streets cover the landfill and the ocean beats many blocks away.

Make **Washington Square Park** your base and branch out from there. If it's the weekend, artists will be out on the grass selling their works. And if it's the weekday, there will still be people out there sunning themselves.

City Lights Bookstore

This is the Italian section of town called **"Little Italy"** by the locals; and in the 1950s, this was where the beatniks congregated.

Vesuvio's

You will find vestiges of both elements as you walk around.

Peek into **City Lights Bookstore**, owned by Lawrence Ferlinghetti and located a few blocks away at Broadway and Columbus. You might want to come back if there is a poetry reading that night. Close by is the other remnant of the Beat days, **Vesuvio's**. Poet Dylan Thomas whiled away many hours in this bar.

There are lots of **open-air cafés** in Little Italy where you can sit and people-watch. When you get hungry, you will be tempted by the many restaurants in this stretch of town. Since it is Italian, I recommend the **Fior d'Italia**, 601 Union, which is virtually a landmark. The food is good and the service wonderful. You might have to wait if you didn't make reservations earlier, however. Ask the waiter to show you the menu from May 1, 1886. Can you imagine paying 15 cents for veal scaloppine?

As the evening draws more into night, walk along **Grant Avenue**. There are lots of bars on this street that play some pretty good music. So be a typical San Franciscan out on the town. Check out the various bars and go back to the one you like the best. This is how you will isolate your favorite hangout, a place you can come back to again and again.

The coffee shop on the corner at Green and Grant is a well-known favorite. Don't forget to look at the pictures on the walls.

Theater

Look in the pink pages of the *San Francisco Chronicle* for listings of the ballet, opera, symphony and the theater (the ACT is particularly good). There is always something going on in San Francisco.

Castro crawl

San Francisco has acquired the reputation of being the gay capital of the world. Yes, there are many gays in this city and yes, they certainly add to the ambience of San Francisco. Nestled in the heart of the gay district is the **Castro Theater**, on Castro Street near Market Street. It is one of the old-time theaters, the sort they don't make any more. Very ornate decorations make it look like a palace. The organ always plays before the movie comes on. So go watch a movie to experience the America of yore. Besides, the theater usually has very good movies, so check the listings and go on a suitable day.

I do not recommend that you end the evening by going to a gay bar. You might become uncomfortable if you go merely to look.

Hornblower Dining Yacht

I am usually not in favor of recommending something that is of the tourist ilk, but the *Hornblower* dining yacht is an exception. On board you can dance to live music and dine on freshly prepared meals. There is something indescribably beautiful about a city at night, particularly if you are seeing it from the water. If you flew into San Francisco at night, you probably looked down upon its spread of fairy tale lights, and if you went up to Twin Peaks at night you probably saw the same, though from much closer. But to see the city while you float by it is an experience you must take back with you. So call 394-8900 to make a reservation and enjoy yourself.

Dancing

There are a number of dance clubs to choose from in San Francisco. Below I list three of my favorites but I suggest you look in the Pink Pages of *The San Francisco Chronicle* to get updates on which group is playing where.

Club O: 278 11th Street, 621-8119. A huge dance emporium complete with indoor/outdoor dance floor and rooftop swimming pool. Dance to a mix of live music and progressive rock DJ selections. Daily 9 p.m. - 2 a.m; Friday and Saturday 9 p.m. - 4a.m.; pool parties on summer Sundays 1 - 8 p.m.

DNA Lounge: 375 11th Street, 626-1409. Dancing every night, 9 p.m. - 2 a.m. The place has an industrial look to it, with lots of mobiles, multi-levels and many, many, dark corners. The music is eclectic modern rock and the crowd is young. Mostly under 30, artsy, punk dancers who wear nose rings and color their hair purple. If you don't want to stand out, wear black and do some mod hopping on the floor.

Club DV8: At 55 Natoma, 957-1730. Dancing Wednesday to Thursday, 9 p.m. - 2 a.m., Friday and Saturday to 4 a.m. The decor is very trendy, with three dance floors. The music is modern rock and the crowd consists of professionals as well as students. The dress style is also trendy and as for the dance style, anything goes. Order their most popular drink, the Long Island Iced Tea. Sometimes there are live shows.

"THE BEST SHOW I'VE EVER SEEN" —Milton Berle

The World Famous

An Evening at La Cage

HILARIOUS

"OUTSTANDING IMPERSONATIONS..."

A FUN, LAVISH, FULL SCALE NIGHTCLUB REVUE
FOR DINNER AND SHOW RESERVATIONS - 391-9999
435 BROADWAY, SAN FRANCISCO

Day Trips

The very setting of San Francisco is ideal. The city is within hours of wonderful parks, beaches and mountains. Here then, is a selection of out-of-town places to visit.

1. Point Reyes National Seashore

What to do before: pack a picnic lunch, put on a pair of walking shoes, don't forget something warm and you will be set for a day at **Point Reyes**. Call **Greens** ($) at 771-6222 to make dinner reservations.

Cross the Golden Gate Bridge and take the **Sir Francis Drake exit**. Just follow this road and in about an hour you will see the information sign for **Point Reyes Headquarters**. This is the quick way of getting there. You will drive along small towns, a golf course, lovely scenery, till you arrive at Point Reyes National Seashore. You will see many stalls selling fresh fruit in season; stop and add to your picnic basket as they taste very good.

As you approach, tune into 1610 AM on your radio to get information about the park. Turn left and into the information center where you can pick up a map and choose a trail. The desk is very helpful and if you can't decide on a trail, tell them what you are looking for and they will help you find it. One of my favorites is the **Sky Trail,** which loops out from the **Bear Valley Trail**. It is a beautiful hike any time of year because of the varied scenery. You will walk past small hills, large meadows filled with flowers in the springtime, clear water creeks, huge conifers and at the very end, like a shimmering trophy, is the sea. At first the sea is just a blue dot but then it grows and grows until you can look down and see the crashing waves, the sand and the cliffs.

Picnic at **Arch Rock**, the cliff that makes you feel you have reached the end of the world. You can feed some bread to the pestering sea gulls and then lie back and enjoy the view. During the whale season – December through March – you can look for spouts that tell you where the mammals are. There is plenty of wildlife in Point Reyes so don't be surprised if you see a small herd of deer, maybe even an albino among them. There are huge squirrels too, so big you might mistake them for rabbits! But don't disturb the animals or the flowers. Take the Bear Valley Trail for the return; it is an easy, mostly downhill, walk.

Further up is a **lighthouse**. The walk down to the lighthouse is fine; but is a long way back to the top. The town of **Inverness** is further on and if you like Point Reyes, this is a good place to base yourself. If you drive as far as Inverness, you might want to consider another hike. Look for the **McClure Beach** sign, and stop at the first outcrop of buildings. This was the stomping ground of tule elk and mountain lions. These two animals once roamed freely in great numbers. Today the elk are slowly making a comeback and if you wish to see them, hike along the headlands on the **Tomales Point Trail** and a seven-mile (11-km) round trip just about guarantees a sighting. But even if you don't see these horned creatures, the walk is fairly easy and the scenery captivating.

When you are ready to drive back, take Highway 1. This is a very scenic route, and you will pass fishing towns and picture-book farms, with almost always a view of the sea. Look for the sign for **Pelican Inn,** close to Muir Beach. This droll eatery features tea and crumpets and beer for those who want something stronger. You can sit outside in the wooden courtyard.

Proceed onto San Francisco and when you see the sign for the **Zen Center**, make a mental note. For in the evening you will dine at **Greens,** which is partly owned by the center. It is not too far from the Golden Gate Bridge and to the left, in **Fort Mason**, Building A. Fresh produce from gardens in Green Gulch forms the basis for their mouth-watering vegetarian cuisine. So even if you are a meat-and-potatoes person, you will be pleased you tried greens for at least one meal. The waterfront dining room is just one of its many plus points.

For steadfast walkers only

2. Napa Valley

What to do before: call Napa Valley Balloons, Inc., 707-253-2224 or 1-800-253-2224, to make a reservation (do so as far in advance as possible); call Dr. Wilkinson's Hot Springs, 707-942-4102 to make an appointment for a mud bath and massage; call Mustards Grill ($$), 707-944-2424, to make dinner reservations. If you like adventure, wine, and being spoilt, this is the day for you.

The balloon company will give you directions on how to get there and the time you have to be there: very early. So you will doubtless have a dark ride to the **Domain Chandon Winery**, the take-off spot for your ride above Napa Valley.

The ride lasts for an hour and you float over vineyards and between the mountains of Napa Valley. The landing occurs where the wind wills. Often the balloon comes to a halt in a vineyard or behind someone's house. Transportation is provided back to Domain Chandon where a champagne brunch awaits. The brunch is picnic style. You will also be given a photograph and a balloon pin.

If, however, you are traveling by car, Napa Valley is about one hour north of San Francisco off Highway 29. Take the Bay Bridge to Highway 80 North; at Vallejo follow the signs to Highway 29.

After brunch, continue down Highway 29 and stop at the **wineries** that catch your fancy. The **Beringer Vineyards** provide a comprehensive tour that tells you all about wine making. The tour begins in the caves that are cut into the hillside and ends in the tasting room. The grounds are extensive and beautiful and many people picnic here. But really, there is no set schedule to follow till you go to your mud bath appointment down the road at Calistoga.

This is a real treat, California style. First you immerse yourself in a mud bath, then you rinse off and soak up the heat in a hot tub, followed by a blanket wrap and, finally, the massage.

Depending on the time, you can either stop at some vineyards, visit **Old Faithful Geyser** or walk through the **Petrified Forest**.

Dinner is at **Mustards**, 7399 Highway 29. It is a popular spot. The atmosphere is casual and chic and the menu very imaginative.

Getting an overview of the vineyards

3. Berkeley

What to do before: call **Chez Panisse**, 548-5049, to make reservations for lunch; call **Skates**, 549-1900, to make reservations for dinner. Make both reservations the same day.

Just across the bay is the university town of Berkeley. Take the Bay Bridge across – yes, the very one which has been re-built since the earthquake, and get off at the University Avenue exit. If you are an early bird, you will see a long line of cars trying to get across to San Francisco. Continue down University Avenue until you reach **Sacramento**, then turn right and look for the **Homemade Café** at 2454 Sacramento Street. Its good food has given it a name in Berkeley. Choose between omelets, excellent muffins, coffee cake, *matzo brei* (Jewish french toast) and *blintzes* with fresh blueberry sauce.

After breakfast, get back on University Avenue and take it all the way till you see green lawns that force you to turn left or right. That is the campus of the **University of California, Berkeley**. It is very difficult to find parking so I suggest you go to the university garage on Telegraph and Bancroft. (To find it, turn right on Oxford Street, take the first left and turn left once more when you reach Telegraph Avenue. Turn left again on Bancroft and look immediately to your right for the pay garage. Bancroft is a one-way street.)

Take the elevator up to the second floor and pick up a brochure at the **Visitor Information Center**. It includes a good map which will guide you all over the campus.

The original design for the campus was by Frederick Law Olmsted, America's first great landscape architect who also designed New York's Central Park. John Galen Howard designed many of the buildings, among them some of California's most famous landmarks: The **Greek Theater**, **Doe Library** (don't forget to admire the ceiling in the Reading Room) and **Sather Tower** (modeled on the bell tower in St. Mark's Square, Venice). You can ride the elevator to the top of the Campanile to get an all-round view of the campus and its environs. Bernard Maybeck, a famous Bay Area architect, designed the Men's Faculty Club and the Hearst Gym.

Berkeley is also known for its militant flower children image of the 1960s. Walk where you wish. Today **Sproul Plaza**, where the Free Speech Movement began in the 1960s, is the place where you can see jugglers, comedians, singers, evangelists and, of course, students. The Polka Dot Man can be found in **Dwinelle Plaza** and look out for the Bubble Lady, who might try and sell you her little book of poems.

Before you take off again, wander down **Telegraph Avenue**. Here you will see street vendors who sell the zaniest things (T-shirts printed Berzerkley) and people with purple hair riding skateboards at top speed.

Lunch is at **Chez Panisse**, in the gourmet section of Berkeley, north of the campus. This world-famous restaurant, owned by Alice Waters, is at 1517 Shattuck Avenue. For the past 12 years she has

set the trends in American cuisine. The menus change daily, but always feature original dishes prepared with organically-grown ingredients and accented with chef Paul Bertolli's Mediterranean flair. Order a dessert. They are unbelievably scrumptious. You can also buy an *Alice Waters cookbook*.

The restaurant is generally booked months in advance, so you will be eating upstairs at the café, which is a more affordable version of the downstairs. If for some reason there is a long wait for lunch, wander along Shattuck and into **Walnut Street Square**. You will encounter the best bread (French Board) the best coffee (Peet's) and a lovely bookstore (Black Oak). Have your aprés-lunch, pick-me-up coffee opposite at the **French Hotel & Café** and if it's a nice day you can sip it sitting outside.

Now head north and follow the signs that say **Tilden Park**. This park was named for the EBRPD's (East Bay Regional Park Development) first president and is the most extensively developed of the East Bay regional parks. The park offers a variety of activities including an archery range, botanic garden, golf course, merry-go-round, miniature railroad, pony rides and tennis courts.

The **Brazilian Room** is a popular place for receptions, so don't be too surprised if you see a wedding entourage as you drive by. Once you pass the Brazilian Room, make a left and keep going till you see a parking lot on your left. This is **Inspiration Point**, where Berkeleyites come to walk or run. It makes a lovely walk; you are in the midst of nature and on a clear day, San Francisco and the Golden Gate Bridge are so close you can almost

touch them. You don't have to stick to the path; branch out or climb a hill. Or you can walk to the **Rotary Peace Monument**. A warning: do not walk the path if it looks isolated. While Berkeley is a safe place, don't take any chances. Don't let the warning discourage you from going there; but make sure there are people there with you.

You can pick up a map of Tilden Park at Inspiration Point and if anything catches your fancy, feel free to explore. The **Steam Trains** are very popular as is sitting around **Lake Anza**.

Dinner is at **Skates**, a glass restaurant on the water. Sitting at a window it is easy to have the illusion that the sailboats are coming right at you.

Take University Avenue and instead of getting on the freeway, continue straight till you come to the Marina and the complex that houses the restaurant.

It's a lovely place for there are sailboats bobbing on the water, the pier to walk on and the Golden Gate Bridge to look at. If you are lucky you will catch the sunset. Read the daily newspaper to see when that will occur and time your visit accordingly. I cannot project a time since America goes on time-saving and the sunset varies widely according to the season. The pier is a good place for an after-dinner walk though it will be extremely windy and chilly. But you can always return to the bar at Skates and get warm again.

Remember that the Bay Bridge gets clogged in the evenings. So you should return to San Francisco as late as possible to avoid the traffic. Leave any time after 8 p.m., keep the $1 toll fare handy and whizz back to your hotel.

Letting off steam at Tilden Park

Fort McDowell

4. Angel Island

What to do before: for times of departure of the daily **Tiburon ferry**, call 435-2131; the ferry from San Francisco runs on weekends and holidays, call 546-2815/2896 for times; call MISTIX at 1-800-444-7275 for information and reservations for campsites.

Angel Island is reached via a ferry from Tiburon. Bikes are a favorite way of getting around the island. Bring along a picnic lunch or if you are with a group, you can make good use of the open-air barbecue pits; bring your own meat and coals.

What Hydra is to Greece, and Venice to Italy, Angel Island is to San Francisco. This one-sq mile (2.6-sq km) park on the largest island in the bay, is free from fumes.

The island, pregnant with the history of the bay area, is not only a haunt for nature buffs. So here are at least two reasons to cross the water to spend the day here.

The ferry will put you at **Ayala Cove**, named after Lt. Juan Manuel de Ayala, reputedly the first European to sail into the bay on his ship the *San Carlos*. Walk towards the green lawn. You should start your stay by visiting the museum. It gives you a quick overview of the island, both botanically and historically.

There are all sorts of hikes you can take but the two most obvious ones are either to go around the island or to climb to the top. I suggest you go for the latter because it takes a shorter time and also because you get some marvellous views.

Ayala Cove

Camp Reynolds

Surrounded by foliage today, it is hard to believe that midway through the 19th century the island was almost devoid of trees. Greenery was brought in, which is why many of the plants and flowers are not native to the land.

The buildings here tell the story of the men who once walked the area. At first the Indians, who lived simply and treated the land with worshipful respect.

The **immigration station** at **Point Simpton** gave the island the sobriquet, "Ellis island of the West". It was the first stop for Asians seeking their fortunes on "Gold Mountain". They were detained here for weeks until authorities ascertained their identities.

Many of them etched poems on the walls that have been collected in a book called *Island*. In 1941, the War Department used the buildings to house German, Italian and Japanese prisoners of war.

When you're through exploring the islands and enjoying the peace and the green, make sure you are in time to catch the ferry back to San Francisco.

Poetry at the immigration station

If there is fog in San Francisco you can be assured that the sun is shining in Santa Cruz. This seaside town, the name of which means **Holy Cross**, is known for its beaches and the boardwalk. Many San Franciscans have a weekend getaway cottage somewhere in Santa Cruz and those who don't, often go down for the sun or the surf.

Santa Cruz is an all-day excursion so have a hearty breakfast. Then

get on Highway 280 and change to Highway 17 in San Jose. The drive will take about two hours and you pass through some wonderful countryside. If it's the weekend, start early to avoid traffic jams.

When you get to Santa Cruz, take Highway 1 North towards the UC Campus. Just follow the signs. When you come to Mission Street, make a detour to the **Mission de Exaltacion de la Santa Cruz.** Turn left instead of right and go to 126 High Street.

Proceed on to the 2000-acre (800-hectare) campus. If you wish you can take a tour but you can just as well drive around to get a feel of this place.

Exit the West Gate and make your way down to the **Lighthouse** on West Cliff Drive. It stands tall and proud at the edge of the sea, recalling a time when ships frequently sailed these seas. **Seal Rock**, home to a herd of sea lions, juts out from the waters, and you can hear and see these melancholy beasts of the sea basking in the sun.

West Cliff Drive

Lunch is at **Crow's Nest**, at 2218 East Cliff Drive. A glass wind breaker keeps you warm as you eat outdoors and watch the yachts come and go. If you do not like seafood you can choose between hamburgers and enchiladas.

After lunch retrace the road you came on till you get to the **Boardwalk**, the place that means Santa Cruz to most people. Today it is a mile-long (1.6-km) entertainment haven, the casino built in 1907 having given over to games for all ages: video games, pinball, shooting galleries, miniature golf, and the rides.

The most well-known is the **Giant Dipper Roller Coaster**, a wooden relic from 1924. The merry-go-round is even older and dates from 1911.

You can walk along the pier and if in season, feed the howling sea lions. I suggest you leave Santa Cruz at 4 p.m. because of traffic jams later. Take

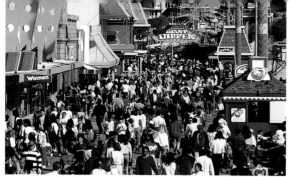
On the Boardwalk

Highway 17 to San Jose and then 280 to San Francisco.

If you wish to stay longer, you can have a delicious seafood dinner on the pier and enjoy the sunset. Be warned, however, that the drive back is very long.

6. Spelunking

What to do before: call (209) 736-2708 or write Cave City Expeditions, P.O. Box 78, Vallecito, CA 95251, to make reservations and to get directions. Vallecito is approximately 3 hours from San Francisco. Cross the Bay Bridge to Oakland, and take Highway 580 east. Watch for signs connecting with Highway 205, then with Route 120. At the town of Sonora, head north on Route 49, then northeast on Route 4.

Wear shabby but warm clothes and rugged shoes with high tops and good friction soles; you will get very muddy and wet so bring towels and clothes to change into afterwards; eat a hearty breakfast, but avoid drinking excessive fluids; bring along a picnic for after spelunking. Make sure you are in good health and not claustrophobic. Hard hats with lights, coveralls and all exploration equipment are provided.

Like Alice, you go into the most magnificent **underground rooms** in the earth. One room looks like a chapel and couples have been married there. The room called **The Womb** will provide an unexpected experience. You squeeze through a small hole into a tiny room. When you are all sitting smashed against each other, switch off your lights and you will have the eerie sensation of being together but alone. Knowledgeable and patient guides will help you while you crawl, slither and hunch-walk, and will continually point out yet another wonder to feast your eyes upon.

For those who have a special interest in unusual places, the **caves** are an insight into a place which has been virtually untouched by human intervention.

Weekend TRiPS

1. Mendocino, a Beautiful Seaside Artists' Colony

What to do before: rent a car; call Gisela Friedman at (707)-937-0866 and ask for the New House; if she is booked, call Mrs. Reeves at (707)-937-5686 and ask for the cottage behind her house, the one with the hot tub. If they both happen to be booked, call Central Reservations at 1-800-262-7801.

Pack good walking shoes and some warm clothes. NB: Mendocino is quite crowded on weekends so if you can, arrange to go during the week.

There are two ways to Mendocino; either take Highway 101 to Highway 1 or take Highway 101 to Highway 128 and then west to Highway 1. Car sickness pills may be required because of curves. If you drive straight through, the pleasant 156-mile (251-km) trip should take you about four hours. If you have the time, you might want to take a picnic lunch and stop along the way.

Pretty, well-preserved 19th-century houses line the street in charming **Mendocino**. (TV buffs can look for the house featured as Jessica's in the TV series *Murder She Wrote*). Cafés and art galleries abound and the sound of the sea is everywhere. The ambience is relaxed and the people are friendly. It is the sort of place you will fall in love with and want to visit again and again.

The Kelly House Historical Museum at 45007 Albion Street offers a close-up look at one home. This restored 1861 house includes a historical library and museum. The museum contains a collection of photographs and watercolors as well as the histories of many buildings in Mendocino.

Mendocino is an artists' town and you should visit some of the many galleries. Here you can set your own pace. You can laze away the day doing nothing but enjoying the air and reading a good book, or you can put on your walking

shoes. The Headland bluffs are suitable for hikes and those with fishing poles can try their luck. There are numerous bait shops in town and you can ask the owners for a tip as to where the fish are biting. From December to March, there is **whale watching** at the **Mendocino Headlands State Park**, though it is possible to spot the spouts from anywhere close to the ocean.

You can also walk along Main Street and branch off to the beach. This is the stretch of sand you saw as you drove into Mendocino. When it gets too warm or windy, you can hide in one of the caves.

If you want something more energetic, go for a hike in **Van Damme Park** to your left just before you get to Mendocino. Further south, where the leached soil has produced miniature trees, is **Pygmy Forest**.

I recommend **Café Beaujolais** especially for breakfast. But get there early (about 8 a.m.) to ensure a seat. It is very popular.

Coffee à la Beaujolais

2. Lake Tahoe

What to do before: call 1-800-AT TAHOE to make reservations; if it's winter call (916) 577-3550 for road and weather conditions.

Tahoe is 195 miles (314 km) from San Francisco and is a four-hour drive. Take Highway 80 and then Highway 50 all the way to the lake. The **Nut Tree** is along the way and is a pleasant place to stop, which children especially like because of its model train. There is good food and the gift shop carries interesting items. Those of you on the hunt for presents can take home some peanut brittle.

There are many stories attached to Lake Tahoe. One legend has it that as an American Indian was being chased by an evil spirit, the Indian had a magical tree branch with him. He dropped the branch, which created a huge water hole: Lake Tahoe. The spirit, unable to traverse the water, had to go around it. The Indian continued running but the fiend gained on him. The monster was almost at his heels when the Indian dropped a leaf and behind him appeared **Fallen Leaf Lake**.

Nestled in the Sierras, Lake Tahoe shares its bounty between Nevada and California. It is the largest and the deepest lake in the mountains and the second largest alpine lake in the world. It is also one of the most beautiful lakes, with clear pristine waters.

Lake Tahoe is divided between either North Lake Tahoe or South Lake Tahoe. I recommend the former because it is more peaceful and, I think, prettier. But you can circumnavigate the lake and choose where you would rather spend your time.

During the summer there is swimming, hiking, boating, tennis, bicycling, horseback riding, river rafting, camping, fishing, water-skiing and backpacking. If you stay in the North side, walk along the road and look for trails that lead to tiny isolated beaches. You can also drive around and look at ostentatious summer homes, often with lavish and beautifully decorated interiors. The **Donner Memorial State Park,** two miles (3.2 km) west of Truckee on Highway 40, is a monument to the Donner Party, who were stranded here during the winter of 1846. They are remembered best for having survived by resorting to cannibalism. The **Ponderosa Ranch** is a must for those who grew up watching *Bonanza* on TV.

There is no need to give directions for gambling. Casinos are easily found on the Nevada side.

Fallen Leaf Lake is close by and is not as crowded as Tahoe. It is much smaller but just as stunning. You can rent a boat and do the waters or take an easy hike to nearby waterfalls.

During the winter Tahoe puts away its sparkling blue and green and brings out the white for its visitors' better entertainment. You can stay at a number of resorts, such as **Alpine Meadows** (phone 916-583-4232, snow phone 916-583-6914); **Boreal** (phone 916-426-3666, snow phone 916-426-3663, accommodations 916-426-3668); **Donner Ski Ranch** (phone 916-426-3635, accommodations 916-426-3622); **Granlibakken** (phone 916-583-4242, snow phone 916-583-9896, accommodations 1-800-543-3221); **Heavenly** (phone 916-541-1330, snow phone 916-541-7544, accommodations 1-800-288-2463); **Kirkwood** (phone 209-258-6000, snow phone 209-258-3000, accommodations 1-800-967-7500); and **Sierra Ski Ranch** (phone 916- 659-7535, snow phone 916-659-7475, accommodations 1-800-AT-TAHOE).

Those interested in cross-country skiing should try **Tahoe Nordic** (phone 916-583-0484; accommodations 1-800-824-6348) and **Tahoe Donner Cross-Country** (phone 916-587-9484; accommodations 1-800-824-6348).

3. Yosemite

What to do before: call 209-252-4848 for information and reservations for accommodations; call 1-800-365-2267 for recorded information on camping. Call 209-372-0200 for information on roads and weather conditions.

Yosemite National Park is located about 210 miles (338 km) from San Francisco, approximately a four-hour drive. Take Highway 80 to Highway 580 to Highway 205 and then to Highway 120. During winter you might want to take Highway 140 from Merced.

Along the way you could make a stop at the **Hershey Chocolate Company** at 120 South Sierra Avenue, Oakdale. You can take a half-hour tour, the end of which is concluded with something sweet from the factory.

It is possible to "do" Yosemite National Park in a day but that

The Mirror Lake

would be rushing it. Why breeze through a place Ansel Adams spent his life photographing, a park so haunting that most people wish they had come sooner and leave determined to visit again?

Yosemite is popular any time of year. "Don't litter" is the catch phrase for a trip to Yosemite. People go to climb, others to hike and ride horses, while others prefer to camp there.

Yosemite was designated a National Park in 1890 and today it embraces 1,169 sq miles (2,600 sq km) of parkland. Its eastern boundary is the **Sierra Nevada mountains**. The **Merced** and the **Toulumne** rivers that water the park originate in the snowy peaks of that mountain range.

Yosemite has something to offer no matter what the season is, but during winter its vibrancy is lost beneath the white snow. The snow has an enchantment all its own but you will miss out on the colors that make the park look like an artist's palette from afar.

Tuolumne Meadows

There are at least two ways of doing Yosemite: by car or on foot. For the former you should take the **Tioga Pass Road,** which traverses the park and is the eastern entrance. The first 12 miles (19 km) of this two-lane paved road ascend for about a mile (1.6 km) and overlook a huge canyon.

Then the road winds through **Tuolumne Meadows** down to **Tenaya Lake**. The drive provides a good overview of the park and should whet your appetite so that you will want to see more.

View from Olmstead Point

If you are going on foot, put on a day pack and choose from a variety of trails. There are various **Visitors' Centers** whose staff will be more than pleased to help you find a suitable trail. This is the only way to feel the power and splendor of the park. Two easy hikes are to **Bridalveil Falls** and the **Lower Yosemite Falls**. The former gets its name from the spray that makes it look like a bride's veil.

There are other hikes to **Glacier Point**, **Half-Dome** and **Mirror Lake Loop**. But make the most of the services of the Center so that you know all the available routes to choose from. Be confident, however, that any hike you choose will not let you down. You can also go on a tour to all the interesting spots in Yosemite Valley.

In winter, you can ski, cross-country ski or skate. **Badger Pass,** opened in 1935, is the oldest organized ski area in California. It is a good place for beginners and very popular with families.

Cross-country skiing can be arranged via the **Mountaineering School**, phone 209-372-1244). For downhill skiing in Badger Pass, call 209-454-2000 for accommodations. The number is 209-372-1330 and the snow phone is 209-372-1338. This is a small resort with slopes that are ideal for beginners and less experienced skiers.

The Yosemite Falls

4. Carmel

What to do before: contact the Tourist Information Center, P.O. Box 7430, Carmel, CA 93921, phone (408) 624-1711 to make lodging arrangements. Carmel is very popular so try to make reservations as far in advance as you can.

Carmel is approximately 2 hours south of San Francisco. Take Highway 1 (alternatively, Highway 280 to 17 to 1) down the coast past Monterey. Like Yosemite, it is possible to make Carmel a hurried one-day trip. But the advantages of a weekend stay go beyond the five-hour round-trip drive. The best you can do on this trip is to enjoy Carmel at leisure and use it as a base to explore the exquisite **Monterey Peninsula**.

Of late the charming seaside town of Carmel made front page news when actor Clint Eastwood ran for mayor and won. But long before that, back in 1904, a number of artists and writers had cultivated this retreat. As more and more people discovered it, the founders fought against modernization in the form of paved streets, gas and electricity. These early efforts have preserved the quaint and village-like ambience of Carmel, clearly evident in the architecture of the houses.

It is a lovely place to wander about in. The streets are clean and the shops very interesting, with galleries and bakeries, bookstores and restaurants. When you tire of walking head for the beach at the end of the road. The soft white sand makes the **Carmel City Beach** a stunning study as it fans out against the deep blue of the Pacific Ocean. Try to catch a sunset. **River Beach,** south of Carmel, is not as popular but if you do go there, stop off at **Tor House**. Poet Robinson Jeffers built it in 1919 using boulders from the beach.

The **Mission San Carlos Borromeo Del Rio Carmelo**, known simply as the Carmel Mission, is at 3080 Rio Road. One of the 21 California missions, it was founded in 1770 in Monterey by Father Junipero Serra and was moved here in 1771 and used by Father Serra as his

Ocean Avenue shopping

Mission San Carlos Borromeo Del Rio Carmelo

residence and head-quarters till his death in 1784. He is buried at the foot of the altar.

Some of his books and documents are on display in the museum, along with **Indian artifacts**, mission tools, re-creations of the original kitchen and California's very first library.

There is a lovely garden. The cemetery has simple graves out-lined with abalone shells. The church is very popular for wed-dings and services so don't be disappointed if you cannot enter.

Just south of Carmel, on Route 1, is **Point Lobos Reserve**, a 1,325-acre (500-hectare) state-run sanctu-ary. This rugged seacoast has the Monterey cypress, wild flowers, sea lions, sea otters, pelicans and the ever-screeching gulls. Trek to the edge and look at anemones, big fish and wonderful shells in the tide pools. If you walk along the interior trails, keep an eye out for poison ivy.

A stay in Carmel is not complete unless you do the famous **17- Mile Drive** at **Pebble Beach**. Exit off Highway 1 between Monterey and

Detail of the Mission

Carmel. The road winds around expensive homes, pres-tigious golf courses and in-credible seascapes. You will be given a map at the toll booth which will help you place Rest-less Sea, Seal and Bird Rock and the Lone Cypress. During the season, seals give birth here. Visitors are cautioned not to get too close. You can make this a whole-day trip and bring along a picnic.

Just north of Carmel is

Along the 17-Mile Drive

Monterey, a town which used to be the capital of Alta California under the Spanish, Mexican and American flags. Today it serves as an all-year playground for the rich with several golf courses, a beach and the **Monterey State Historic Park**.

The first and most popular stop is **Fisherman's Wharf.** The wharf was built it in 1846 by convicts, military deserters and native American Indians and for years it docked one of the largest fishing and whaling fleets in the west. Today there are more shops than fishermen but it is still enjoyable to battle against the wind as you walk along the wharf. Sea lions congregate around the pilings begging for fish, so be generous.

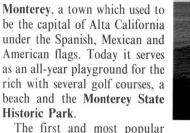

Cannery Row is the inspiration for two of John Steinbeck's famous novels, *Cannery Row* and *Sweet Thursday*. In 1945 sardines suddenly disappeared from the sea and in their wake followed the once booming sardine canneries. Today the mile-long road still offers fish, but it is served in the many restaurants that line the streets. There are art galleries and a Historical Wax Museum. The latter has a slide show of old Monterey.

The prized possession of Cannery Row is the **Monterey Bay Aquarium**, one of the largest aquariums in the world with nearly 300 species of marine life from 23 major habitat areas. There is a 90-foot (27-meter) re-creation of Monterey Bay, a two-storey sea otter tank, a three-storey kelp forest, a hands-on tide pool, a shorebird aviary, a theater and life-size models of marine animals.

Look out for the **Monterey Jazz Festival** in September. In October, drive to **Pacific Grove** to witness the return of the **Monarch butterflies**. They migrate here every year from Canada and stay until March before flying north again. These fluttering, beautiful creatures are a mystery because, with a life span of less than a year, it is impossible for one butterfly to make the trip twice.

The Great Tide Pool (above) and the Kelp Forest (right)

Dining

San Francisco is a gourmet's delight, a city that pleases the stomach as much as the eye and heart. The rich blend of ethnic cultures is most evident in the varied restaurants. On one street alone you can choose between Hunan, Cantonese, Vietnamese, Italian, American and French cuisines, to name just a few. Choosing from these numerous restaurants can almost make one dizzy.

For your convenience, I have listed the restaurants and their specialities. Price gauge: $ = < $10; $$ = > $10; $$$ = > $20.

Breakfast

Postrio, 545 Post St., 776-7825 ($$)
One of the "in" places. Breakfast here ranges from corned beef hash topped with poached eggs and Hollandaise sauce to muffins, scones, granola and porridge. Invariably crowded, no reservations, so you'll have to beat the crowd.

Kuleto's, 221 Powell St., 397-7720 ($)
Good service and excellent food. Waiters are quick and solicitous, the eggs are prepared just so and their fresh fruit *focaccia* is truly and uniquely good.

The Boudin Sourdough Bakery, Fisherman's Wharf

Il Fornaio at Levi Plaza, 1265 Battery St., 986-0100 ($)
Everything is good, from their coffee to their Calzoncino del Mezzadero (a turnover filled with eggs, sausage, onion and potatoes) to the view (trees and a fountain). If you like it enough to come back for dinner, order any claypot dish.

Doidge's, 2217 Union St., 921-2149 ($)
This is a home breakfast with a vengeance. The food reminds you of a meal in a farmhouse and includes 10 types of bread and honey-cured bacon and ham. Two specialities for hearty eaters: a casserole of Italian sausage, potatoes, onions and tomatoes topped with cheese and either sour cream or poached egg, and baked eggs wrapped in bacon and flavored with pimiento and vermouth.

Home Plate, 2274 Lombard St., 922-4663 ($)
Pick from about 30 fillings, among them roasted chicken, homemade pork-dill sausage and smoked salmon with onions for omelets. Other dishes include waffles with genuine maple syrup and potato-carrot pancakes.

Zuni Café, 1658 Market St., 552-2522 (Closed Monday) ($)
The café does not feature a large menu but what it does offer is first-class. You must have the Acme bread.

Harbor Village Restaurant, 4 Embarcadero Center, 781-8833 ($$)
Get here before 11 a.m. to enjoy unforgettable dim sum.

Royal Kitchen, 3253 Mission St., 824-4219 (closed Tuesday) ($)
This restaurant gives you reason not to avoid the Mission. Dim sum and pot stickers, all cooked to perfection.

Benkay, Nikko Hotel, Mason and O'Farrell streets, 394-1100. ($$)

Traditional Japanese breakfast is at Cafe 222 on 2nd floor; lunch and dinner in Benkay on the 25th floor, the view is breathtaking.

Crusty's Sourdough Café, Sir Francis Drake, Sutter and Powell streets, 392-7755. ($$)

The decor is 1920s San Francisco. Come here for sourdough bread for a breakfast San Francisco style.

Brunch

Crown Room, Atop the Tower, Fairmont Hotel, 950 Mason, 772-5131. ($$$)

The hotel was featured in the TV series *Hotel*. The breakfast brunch every Sunday from 10.00 a.m. - 2.30 p.m. must be eaten to be believed.

Top of the Mark, Mark Hopkins Inter-Continental, California and Mason streets, 392-3434. ($$$)

The Sunday buffet brunch from 10 a.m. - 2 p.m. has become a tradition among San Franciscans. Impress your guests with the food and the view.

Lunch

Vicolo Pizzeria, 900 North Point, 776-1331. ($)

This restaurant has a special pizza that is really worth trying. For those who want something light there is salad.

Tadich Grill, 240 California St., 391-2373. ($$)

One of the few restaurants in the city that does not accept reservations. People line up outside. A veritable San Francisco establishment. Owned by Yugoslavians, it has been serving the best seafood for decades. The waiters do a wonderful job of deboning the fish.

Mind your step at the Beaujolais Café

Panos, 4000 24th St., 824-8000. ($)
Greek food. Sit at a table spread with a clean white tablecloth and watch the world go by.

Pauli's Café, 2500 Washington, 921-5159. ($)
Come here for a light lunch of salads and sandwiches.

Max's Opera Café, 601 Van Ness Ave., 771-7300. ($)
Huge sandwiches are served so come only if very hungry.

Sparky's, 242 Church St., 621-6001. ($)
It specializes in pizza but also serves American diner foods such as hamburgers.

Spuntino, 524 Van Ness Ave., 861-7772. ($)
Italian, serves salads, homemade pasta, breads and pizzas cooked in a wood-fired oven.

La Mediterranée, 2210 Fillmore St., 921-2956. ($)
Middle-Eastern, order pitta bread and *hummus* for starters.

Cinderella Bakery, Delicatessen and Restaurant, 436 Balboa Street, 751-9690. ($)
Marvellous Russian food. Try their *piroshki*, the *baorhch* and the *pelemeni*.

Dinner

MacArthur Park, 607 Front St., 398-5700. ($$)
Think MacArthur Park and you will think of oakwood-smoked baby back ribs. But equally famous is its mesquite grilled fresh fish and dry-aged steaks.

California Culinary Academy, California Hall, 625 Polk Street, 771-3500. Closed on weekends. ($$$)
Students cook and serve during in-school training. The foods are masterpieces of sight and taste.

Stars, 150 Redwood, 861-7827. ($$$)
Yet another "in" place in San Francisco. Excellent food though rather noisy.

Bangkok Express, 907 Irving, 681-1288. ($)
An upscale Thai restaurant. The waitresses dress in their native costumes and the food is authentic.

PJ's Oyster Bed, 737 Irving, 566-7775. ($$)
A noisy eatery. Sit at the counter or at tables. The catch is very fresh. The food is prepared in an open kitchen.

Dungeness Crabs

Swan Oyster Depot, 1517 Polk, 673-1101. ($)
This restaurant is part of the San Francisco eating experience. It has a limited menu but go there for really fresh oysters (8 a.m. - 5.30 p.m.).

Jack's Restaurant, 615 Sacramento, 421-7355. ($$)
One of the older restaurants in San Francisco, it gets added publicity because of Herb Caen's newspaper column.

Capp's Corner, 1600 Powell, 989-2589. ($$)
An Italian family-style restaurant with a fixed menu and enormous servings. Noisy but fun.

Basque Hotel & Restaurant, 15 Romolo Place, 788-9404. ($$)
Another family-style restaurant with large portions.

The Fog City Diner, 1300 Battery, 982-2000. ($$)
Well-known for its mostly American cuisine and its setting – a railroad car. The atmosphere is great.

Washington Square Bar and Grill, 1707 Powell, 982-8123. ($$)
Local and out-of-town artists and politicians dine here. So everyone comes to see, be seen, and eat. Good pasta and great steaks.

The Balboa Café, 3199 Fillmore, 922-4595. ($$)
Come here for burgers and salads. There is a good wine selection as well.

Buca Giovanni, 800 Greenwich, 776-7766. ($$)
Authentic Italian food, specializing in Tuscan dishes; well-known for its fresh game and home-grown herbs.

There are numerous shopping arcades and malls in San Francisco to cater to your every need and whim. Furthermore, there are unique shopping tours which even bring you out of town to converted warehouses filled to the rafters with discount designer clothes. Each shopping spree can be tailored to suit each individual style, schedule and budget. For some of these tours, look under "Tours" in the What To Know section of this book.

The following suggestions refer to a selection of shopping centers and areas in the city:

San Francisco Shopping Center

This nine-storey Italian marble, green granite-and-glass mall is just three blocks from Union Square at Fifth and Market. Opened in late 1988, the $140-million building has 100 shops and six spiral escalators, while the top five floors feature a novel store-in-the-sky. Nature lovers will enjoy the atrium covered with a retractable skylight. (Powell Street BART and Muni Station are at the concourse level; the cable car station is above.)

Crocker Galleria

Teddybears at FAO Schwartz

Crocker Galleria

The building, located at Sutter and Montgomery, is modelled after the Galleria Vittorio Emanuele in Milan. The wonderful glass dome hovers above 50 shops and restaurants. Boutiques on the pavilion carry the best of both American and European designers. Shop here if you want to wear something unique. (Parking is at the Sutter Street entrance.)

Embarcadero Center

In the old days this used to be the site of the produce market. Later, a shopper's paradise emerged. One can get lost trying to get from One Embarcadero Center to Five Embarcadero Center. There are waterfalls, and outdoor cafés to rest one's feet. (Embarcadero Station BART and and garage parking are nearby. Parking is free on Sundays; on Monday to Saturday there is discount parking with validation.)

Japan Center

Minoru Yamasaki designed this huge complex which opened in 1968. The 5 acres (2 hectares) offer restaurants, sushi bars, art galleries, bookstores, theaters, Japanese baths and so on. Don't forget to admire the main entrance before you head in to buy memorabilia from the Orient.

Union Square

Sear's is in the heart of the shopping district so when you are sated, all you have to do is walk out and into any of the big stores around Union Square. The square was named on the eve of the Civil War, when it was the site of many pro-Union meetings. The famous **St. Francis Hotel** stands on one side of the square and is framed by the famous shopping havens of **Saks Fifth Avenue**, **Burberry's of London**, **Macy's**, **I. Magnin** and **Neiman Marcus**. Flowers are everywhere and several street corners have flower stands that seem more permanent than temporary.

On various side streets around the square are boutiques like **Gucci**, **Tiffany**, **Jaeger**, **Brooks Brothers**, **Ralph Lauren**, **Celine**, **Pierre Deux**, **Laura Ashley** and **Cartier** – for starters.

FAO Schwartz delights both children and adults. Browse through even if you are not in need of a furry friend. If you don't want to wander into too many stores, go to **Macy's**. The menswear department is across the street. If it is Easter or Christmas, the store goes all out in its decorations with bowers of flowers and singers in period costume.

Nordstrom started out as a shoe store in Seattle but today carries men's and women's wear as well. The store provides a special service to its customers: it will drive you, with your shopping, to your hotel.

Gump's is a must – a treasure place of beautiful Oriental pieces, including a small museum of jade objects.

Meander down **Maiden Lane**, which used to be a premier red-light street of the central Barbary Coast area. Very respectable today, it is filled with cheerful open-air cafés

Fisherman's Wharf

San Franciscans come here because of its color and activity. The shops are interesting to look at. Nobody in San Francisco buys much here except maybe an oyster for a pearl. There are tiers of shops along Pier 39 to Ghirardelli Square. Each shopping complex in the square is uniquely designed. The Cannery used to be the Del Monte fruit packing plant. Now it has a number of shops, gourmet markets, restaurants and art galleries. **Only in San Francisco (AO-1)** sells creative maps that make excellent souvenirs. Enjoy the large ensemble of street shows, from stand-up comedy to animal routines to the statue man who never seems to blink. San Franciscans will tell you to bypass the shops along Jefferson Street and ignore the rickshaw riders. Validated parking.

The Cannery, Fisherman's Wharf

Kite shop, Sausalito

North Beach

Also known as the Italian Section. You must visit the **City Lights Bookstore**, a remnant of the beatnik era, and **Vesuvio's**, a beautiful bar. You might find unexpected discounts of vintage clothing. Traffic jams are common, parking is also a problem. Walk or take a bus.

Chinatown

Silk, embroidered linen, souvenir shops and restaurants line the streets. You can buy anything from cedar chests to the smallest of silk purses. On Grant Avenue are dragon-entwined lamp posts, calligraphy on street signs, and a roofscape of arched eaves and filigreed balconies. Even the phone booths look Chinese and the Big Mac sign is written in Chinese.

Giant fortune cookies, Chinatown

What to Know!

Practical Information

When to visit

San Francisco differs from the beach-and-sun reputation of the rest of California and often surprises summer visitors with its standard cool weather. Visitors still haven't learned that however, and come in droves starting in June. For the sake of their torrential numbers alone, avoid San Francisco during the summer.

Come instead in spring (March, April) when the flowers are blooming or fall (September, October) when it is crisp and the last blooms of summer still perfume the air.

Visas

Most visitors entering the U.S. must possess a valid passport and a visitor's visa. If they arrive from, or have passed through, an infected area, a health certificate is required.

Canadian citizens entering from the Western Hemisphere or Mexican citizens who possess border passes do not need visas or passports. Like the visitor's visa, extensions of stay are limited to six months. The visitor may not accept employment during his stay. Do not bring any agricultural products into California.

Clothing

There is almost always a nip in the air, so bring something warm, even if you are visiting during the summer months. Women are most comfortable with a light jacket or coat handy, or in a suit. Men require light-to-medium-weight suits or sports clothes. An all-weather coat is recommended for the evenings and late afternoons.

Electricity

The standard rating is 110 V.

GETTING ACQUAINTED

Geography

Often called the City of Seven Hills, San Francisco actually has some 40 hills, each with its own charm. This Port of Gold that people rushed to from across the ocean and the continent of North America is a compact 47 sq miles (122 sq km).

It is surrounded on three sides by the Pacific Ocean and the San Francisco Bay, and is connected to Marin by the Golden Gate Bridge and to the East Bay by the Bay Bridge.

"The City", as it is called, has a population of 723,959 though it has earned its sobriquet "Everybody's Favorite City" by hosting over eight million tourists, conventioneers and business travelers each year.

Aside from its ideal location for those who love the water, San Francisco has the enviable advantage of having easy access to the mountains (Tahoe), the wilderness (Point Reyes, Yosemite, Sequoia Park) and beaches (Stinson close by and Carmel down the coast). Often mistaken as the capital of California, the title belonging to Sacramento, San Francisco remains the city most people dream of visiting, or better yet, inhabiting.

Climate

San Francisco has a temperate marine climate and enjoys mild weather year-round. Temperatures seldom rise above 70°F (21°C) or fall below 40°F (5°C). Average daytime temperatures: 60°F (15.6°C).

Winter is the wet season, rain falling intermittently from November through March. The dry season falls between June and October.

The most persistent factor remains the fog, which can gray a morning, transform evening into night and bring on the lonely booms of fog horns over the bay. But the fog rarely persists and is usually burned away by the sun by mid-day. So weather-wise, any time is good to visit San Francisco.

Weather Information

To get the most up-to-date information about the weather dial 936-1212.

Time Zone

Pacific. DST. Dial POPCORN to get the exact time.

Tipping

San Francisco may be a small city, but it is big on social etiquette. Service (such as those provided by waiters, hairdressers, and cab drivers) is rewarded with 15 percent of the bill. Most coffee shops have a mug next to the cash register that depends more on generosity than on expectation. Bell boys and valets usually receive two dollars, the maid one dollar, but this too depends on the individual and the service provided.

Tourist Information

The San Francisco Visitor Information Center is located on the lower level of Hallidie Plaza at Market and Powell streets, open weekdays 9 a.m. - 5.30 p.m., Saturday until 3 p.m., Sunday 10 a.m. - 2 p.m. Or you can call their multi-lingual staff at 391-2000. You can also phone 24 hours a day at 391-2001 for a recorded message listing daily events and activities.

For similar information in French, dial 391-2003; German, 391-2004; Spanish, 391-2122; and Japanese, 391-2101.

The Passport Information Center also provides recorded information; call 744-4444.

GETTING AROUND

Taxis

Taxis provide a reasonable and convenient alternative to public transportation. Taxi fares are approximately $3.50 for the first mile and $1.80 for each additional mile. The approximate fare from the airport to the downtown area is $30. Taxis are not difficult to flag down; just hail them from the sidewalk. You can also call for a taxi. Look in the yellow pages of the phone book for extensive listings. A few companies are listed below:

Veteran's Taxicab Company, 552-1300
De Soto Cab Company, 673-1414
Yellow Cab, 626-2345
City Cab, 468-7200

Cars

A large number of agencies offer car rental services in San Francisco. No attempt to quote rates is made here because rental charges are determined by the make and model of the vehicle, length of rental time, day of the week and the amount of service rendered. Rates range from $25 a day to $360. It is advisable to have auto insurance in the U.S. The following agencies are the most centrally located; check the telephone directory for additional offices.

Alamo Rent-a-car, 687 Folsom St., 882-9440

Avis Rent-a-car, 675 Post St., 885-5011, 1-800-331-1212
Budget Rent-a-car, 321 Mason St., 775-5800, 1-800-527-0770
Hertz Rent-a-car, 433 Mason St., 771-2200, 1-800-654-3131

Public Transport (Buses, BART, MUNI)

San Francisco has one of the highest per capita transit riderships in the U.S. because of the largely reliable **San Francisco Municipal Railway**, called **MUNI** by the locals. The fare is $1, except on cable cars where the fare is $3. Exact change is required and free transfers are valid for two changes of vehicle within 90 minutes. Route information is published in the Yellow Pages or may be obtained by calling 673-MUNI. Maps and timetables are rarely on the buses/trolleys themselves; instead, check the bus shelters or buy them at convenience stores such as Walgreen's, Safeway, etc.

Bay Area Rapid Transit (BART) is a fleet of trains that links eight stations in San Francisco with Daly City and 25 stations in the East Bay. Trains operate seven days a week, 6 a.m. to midnight, except on Sundays when service begins at 9 a.m. Tickets are dispensed from machines at the stations. Everything is computerized, fast and clean. Call 788-BART for more information. **AC Transit** operates a bus service to communities in the East Bay – Berkeley, Oakland, Treasure Island – via the San Francisco-Oakland Bay Bridge. Call 510-839-2882 for operator assistance on routes, schedules and fares.

The Golden Gate Transit, 332-6600, links San Francisco to Marin and Sonoma counties via the Golden Gate

Bridge. Call for information on routes, schedules and fares.

SamTrans, 1-800-660-4287, offers a bus service from San Francisco to the San Francisco International Airport and to communities on the Peninsula as far south as Palo Alto.

Caltrain provides rail service to the Peninsula. Call 557-8661 for details.

from Pier 43½ for Sausalito and Tiburon. Fares are $5 for adults, $3 for children. **Angel Island** ferry service operates from San Francisco and Vallejo. Ferries depart from Pier 43½ daily in the summer and week-ends only in the winter. The fare is $10 round trip. Call 546-2700 for more information.

Angel Island and Tiburon are also linked by the **Angel Island State Park** ferry. Call 435-2131 for information.

Ferries

Once some 50 ferries plied the Bay, today, just two companies provide that service. The **Golden Gate Ferries** depart from the south end of the Ferry Building to Sausalito and Larkspur. Call 332-6600 for schedules and fares since they vary depending on the day. The **Red & White Fleet** departs daily

Maps

The San Francisco Convention and Visitors Bureau at Hallidie Plaza, Market and Powell streets, puts out a comprehensive map of San Francisco. Maps — both fun and practical ones — are available at book stores throughout the city. Your hotel will also provide you with a map.

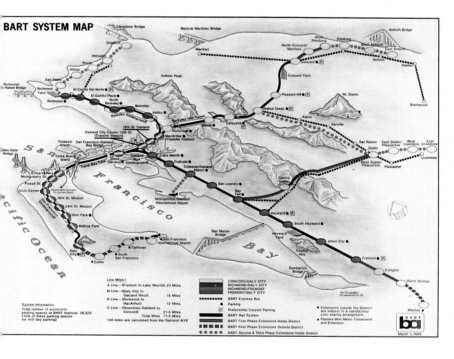

Hotels

Hotels are notoriously expensive in cities and San Francisco is no exception. The ones listed below are most likely to enhance your experience of being in the city. Many of those listed below are old and venerable establishments, while others are included for their good service and price.

When you call up the reservations desk, ask if the hotel has package deals or corporate rates. Sometimes a hotel which advertises $150 per night single occupancy can offer a deal for three nights at the same price. The rates also depend on the season; summer is always busy and prices go up. The hotels have been rated as follows: $ = <100; $$ = >100; $$$ = >200.

The above price categories are based on the lowest rate the hotel charges per night per person. The reservation deposit requirement often means a credit card number. If, for some reason, the following hotels do not suit you, call the **San Francisco Central Hotel Reservation Service** at 1-800-333-8996.

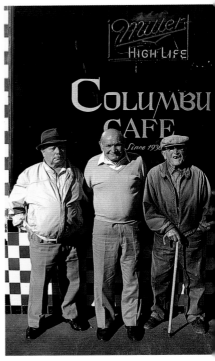

Downtown Listings

$$$

Campton Place Kempinski Hotel
340 Stockton St.
CA 94108
Tel: 781-5555

Four Seasons Clift Hotel
495 Geary St.
CA 94102
Tel: 775-4700

Mark Hopkins Hotel
1 Nob Hill
CA 94108
Tel: 392-3434

The Stanford Court Hotel
905 California St.
CA 94108
Tel: 989-3500
On Nob Hill with stupendous views.

$$

The Donatello
501 Post St.
CA 94102
Tel: 441-7100

Fairmont Hotel & Tower
950 Mason St.
CA 94106
Tel: 772-5000

Holiday Inn
480 Sutter St.
CA 94108
Tel: 398-8900

Hyatt Hotel
345 Stockton St.
CA 94108
Tel: 398-1234

Hyatt Regency
5 Embarcadero Center
CA 94111
Tel: 788-1234

ANA Hotel
50 Third St.
CA 94103
Tel: 974-6400

Petite Auberge
863 Bush St.
CA 94108
Tel: 928-6000
French Country Inn ambience.

Ramada Hotel
590 Bay St.
CA 94133
Tel: 885-4700

San Francisco Hilton & Tower
333 O'Farrell St.
CA 94102
Tel: 771-1400
Close to Union Square.

Sir Francis Drake Hotel
450 Powell St.
CA 94102
Tel: 392-7755

The Westin St. Francis
335 Powell St.
CA 94102
Tel: 397-7000
Renowned.

White Swan Inn
845 Bush St.
CA 94108
Tel: 775-1755

$

Holiday Inn
750 Kearny St.
CA 94108
Tel: 433-6600

Chancellor Hotel
433 Powell St.
CA 94102
Tel: 362-2004

The Raphael
386 Geary St.
CA 94102
Tel: 986-2000

Northern Region

$$$

Miyako Hotel
1625 Post St.
CA 94115
Tel: 922-3200
Authentic Japanese decor.

$$

Inn at the Opera
333 Fulton St.
CA 94102
Tel: 863-8400

Sheraton Hotel
2500 Mason St.
CA 94133
Tel: 362-5500
A block and a half from Fisherman's
Wharf.

$

Kyoto Inn-Best Western
1800 Sutter St.
CA 94115
Tel: 921-4000
Just one block from Japan Center.

Queen Anne Hotel
1590 Sutter St.
CA 94109
Tel: 441-2828
Restored Victorian building, some
rooms have fireplaces.

Stanyan Park Hotel
750 Stanyan St.
CA 94117
Tel: 751-1000
Remodeled Victorian building.
Great view of Golden Gate Park.

Southern Region

$$

San Francisco Airport Hilton
PO Box 8355, CA 94125
(Airport entrance)
Tel: 589-0770
Airport transportation.

$

Radisson Inn
275 South Airport Blvd.
CA 94080
Tel: 873-3550
Airport transportation.

Best Western El Rancho Inn
1100 El Camino Real, Millbrae
CA 94030
Tel: 588-2912
Airport transportation.

Best Western Grosvenor Airport Inn
380 South Airport Blvd.
CA 94080
Tel: 873-3200
Senior discount and airport trans-
portation.

Holiday Inn Crowne Plaza
600 Airport Blvd.
Burlingame, CA 94010
Tel: 340-8500
Overlooks the Bay.

**Holiday Inn San Francisco Interna-
tional**
245 South Airport Blvd,
CA 94040
Tel: 589-7200
Airport transportation.

San Francisco Airport Marriott
1800 Old Bayshore Highway
CA 94010
Tel: 692-9100
Airport transportation.

Sheraton Inn-Airport
1177 Airport Blvd.,
Burlingame, CA. 94010
Tel: 342-9200
Airport transportation.

Bed and Breakfast

A more personalized alternative to a
hotel. **Bed & Breakfast International**,
415-696 1690 or 1-800-872 4500,
P.O. Box 282910, S.F., CA 94128-
2910, can make arrangements for
private rooms in and around San
Francisco.

FINANCIAL SERVICES

Should your credit card be lost or stolen, call American Express at 1-800-528-2121 and Discover Card at 1-800-347-2683; for Mastercard or VISA cards, contact your bank.

Foreign currency exchange is available at the Bank of America, both at the airport (742-8050) and downtown (622-2451). These services are also provided by Citicorp Foreign Currency Exchange at 952-1476 and Deak International at 362-3452.

For lost or stolen travelers checks call American Express at 1-800-221-7282; Bank America at 1-800-227-3460; and VISA at 1-800-227-6811.

BUSINESS HOURS

Business hours are 9 a.m. to 5 p.m., Monday to Friday. Banking hours vary and some banks, like shops, offer limited Saturday service.

HEALTH AND EMERGENCIES

Health care is very expensive in the U.S. You are advised to arrange for health insurance before you come to San Francisco.

The following is a list of offices providing medical, dental and optical care:

Access Health Care, 565-6600; drop-in medical care and health services. You do not need an appointment or be a member.

American Aeromedical, 593-1901; medical, dental, legal and security assistance on a worldwide basis, including hospitalization, medical evacuation and repatriation.

The Medical Center at the University of California, San Francisco, 476-1000; primary and speciality medical services including general acute care, psychiatric, obstetric, dental, children's and 24-hour emergency care available to the public.

PUBLIC HOLIDAYS

New Year's Day: January 1
Martin Luther King's Birthday: January 15 (observed on the following Monday)
Abraham Lincoln's Birthday: February 12; **George Washington's Birthday**: Third Monday in February. Both are observed on **President's Day**, third Monday in February
Memorial Day: Last Monday in May
Independence Day: July 4
Labor Day: First Monday in September
Admission Day: September 9
Columbus Day: Second Monday in October
Veterans Day: November 11
Thanksgiving: Fourth Thursday in November
Christmas: December 25

St. Francis Memorial Hospital, 775-4321; ClinicCARE provides urgent care service 8 a.m. - 5 p.m. Monday to Friday, no appointment. Physicians referral service, 353-6566; Center for Sports Medicine, 353-6400; Emergency Room 353-6300.

San Francisco Ambulance Service, 931-3900; emergency, paramedic and routine ambulance transportation.

San Francisco Dental Office, 777-5115; comprehensive dental care by appointment, 24-hr emergency service, or call Dentist Referral at 421-1435.

Dr. S.A. Silverstein, O.D., 982-5106; San Francisco's oldest eyewear store offers a large selection of frames as well as eye examinations and contact lenses. Most prescriptions can be filled in one day.

Emergencies

For Police/Fire/Ambulance emergencies, dial 911.

For the Fire Department call 861-8020 and for an ambulance, 931-3900.

AIDS

The San Francisco AIDS hotline is 863-AIDS or call 1-800-FOR-AIDS.

COMMUNICATIONS AND NEWS

Postal and Telex

Hotels usually provide telephone, telegram, mail, telex and FAX facilities. If you wish to mail something on your own, look for large blue mail boxes on street corners. Pull down the handle, check to see when the mail will be picked up and slip in the letter.

Cards within the U.S. require 29-cents stamps, while overseas cards need 49 cents, and postcards take a 20-cents stamp.

For Cablegrams or Telegrams, call 1-800-325-6000.

For Express Mail call 1-800-222-1811; for the Main Post Office call 621-6792 and for Postal Information call 550-6500.

Courier Service is provided by Emery at 1-800-443-6379 and Federal Express, 877-9000.

Media

The major daily newspapers in San Francisco are the *San Francisco Chronicle* in the morning and the *San Francisco Examiner* in the afternoon. The two combine into one large edition on Sunday. This weekend paper includes special sections such as the Pink Pages, which highlight the various sports, entertainment, cultural and artistic events of the week.

The Wall Street Journal, *The New York Times*, the *LA Times* and the *International Herald Tribune* are also easily available either from stands at street corners or in shops.

There are numerous FM and AM stations to choose from on the radio and the TV likewise boasts a large number of channels. Most hotels offer cable TV as well as videos.

SPORTS

Crisp weather and wonderful parks have made San Francisco the mecca for outdoor activities.

Witness joggers who go out sun or fog; or walkers out with their dogs; or cyclists clad in neon colors. Many people have taken up outdoor activities since moving to San Francisco. The benefits are varied; you get fit, you get to enjoy the outdoors and sometimes you get to run past celebrities like Robin Williams who has been known to jog in the Golden Gate Park.

Jogging: You can either step out of your hotel and run the streets – and the hills – or you can go to the Golden Gate Park, which has designated jogging paths. Many young people seem to favor the Marina Green. A note of warning: do not run in isolated areas or in badly-lit areas when it's dark.

Bicycling: You can bike anywhere you like, or you can follow two marked scenic bike routes: one tours Golden Gate Park to Lake Merced, the other runs from the south end of the city across the Golden Gate Bridge to Marin County. Bicycle rental shops line Stanyan Street and Geary Boulevard.

Sailing/Boating: The best views of San Francisco are often enjoyed from the Bay, a sailing ground for both novices and experts. Call 922-0227 to rent a sailboat, take a sailing lesson or charter a yacht. Cass' Rental Marina at 332-6789 only rents sailboats to experienced sailors. Those who want something calmer and more predictable can row in Stow Lake in Golden Gate Park. Call 752-0347.

Fishing: Deep-sea fishing is very popular in San Francisco and catches include salmon, halibut, sea bass and shark. Muny Bait and Sport Shop at 673-9815 offers year-round sportfishing charter boats. Look in the Yellow Pages for other such services; boats anchored near Fisherman's Wharf also offer day trips. You will need a fishing license, warm clothes and sea-sickness pills if you have a queasy stomach.

Tennis: The San Francisco Recreation and Parks Department maintains more than 100 tennis courts throughout the city. All are free and available on a first come, first served basis with the exception of 21 courts located in Golden Gate Park, which charge a nominal fee. For advance reservations on weekends call 753-7101.

The Presidio Golf Course

Golf: San Francisco has some beautiful courses. Check with each course regarding fees and rental equipment. Lincoln Park, 221-9911 affords the most beautiful views, while Gleneagles International Golf Course, 587-2425, is the most difficult. Check the Yellow Pages for other listings.

Baseball: The San Francisco Giants play in Candlestick Park, eight miles (13 km) south of the city via Bayshore Freeway on Route 101. But they might be moving, so call 467-8000.

Football: During the season the 49ers play in Candlestick Park. Call 468-2249.

Horse Racing: Two tracks are close enough to San Francisco to warrant visiting. Golden Gate Fields, 510-526-3020, is in the East Bay and thoroughbred races run from late January to June. Post time is 12:30 p.m. every Wednesday to Thursday, Saturday to Sunday, and 6 p.m. on Fridays. Bay Meadows, 574-7223, is in San Mateo, south of San Francisco. Racing takes place every Wednesday through Sunday from August to January. Post times same as Golden Gate Fields.

Fitness Centers:

The following fitness centers are open to non-members for a daily fee. Ask your hotel for additional information on clubs which allow visitors to use their facilities.

Pinnacle Health Club at 135 Post St., 5th and 6th floors, 781-7343. Facilities include yoga, aerobics, weights, circuit training, jacuzzi, sauna, lockers and showers. Open Monday - Thursday, 6 a.m. - 9 p.m.; Friday 6 a.m. - 8 p.m.; Saturday 8 a.m. - 5 p.m.; Sunday 10 a.m. - 4 p.m.

Bert Gustafson's Conditioning Clinic at 609 Sutter St., 885-2918. Facilities here include weights, cycles, swimming pool, steam sauna, lockers and showers. Open Monday - Friday, 7.30 a.m. - 8 p.m.; Saturday 9 a.m. - 4.30 pm.

Marina Club, 3333 Fillmore St., 563-3333. Offers aerobics, stretch/tone, Tae Kwon Do, weights and Nautilus, Lifecycles, Versaclimbers, sauna and steam rooms, lockers and showers. Open weekdays 6 a.m. - 10 p.m.; weekends 8 a.m. - 6 p.m.

Chinese New Year celebration (Jan/Feb)

A little bit of China in San Francisco. Lots of parades, including a Miss Chinatown contest and dragon dances.

San Francisco International Film Festival (Mar)

The film festival takes place in March and is much looked forward to by movie buffs. The films are shown all over the Bay Area, so if you are interested, be prepared to travel.

Black and White Ball (Spring)

This sumptuous evening is held every two years in spring to raise money for the Symphony. Entire streets are cordoned off while people dressed in black and/or white cavort indoors and in the open air. Plenty of food and music.

Bay to Breakers (May)

This marathon takes place in May and is shown on TV. All sorts of runners turn up for the race: those who are serious and those who come to show off their outrageous costumes.

A la Carte A la Park (Oct)

Held in the Golden Gate Park every October, this eating extravaganza draws huge crowds. Restaurants from all over the city put up stalls for people to wander about from one feast to another. Live music and shows liven things, but the food is the main concern. A truly wonderful way to spend the day.

Exotic Erotic Halloween Ball (Oct)

The biggest Halloween party in the world and as the name implies, this is an evening of black lace and garters. Many go merely to gaze at outrageous costumes. Imagine a man who looks like he is wearing a leopard suit, except that the spots are really painted on. There is dancing and various contests. The latter include a costume contest, a Miss Exotic Erotic Ball contest, and a Mr. All American Hunk contest. Those who don't wish to dance can enjoy the many shows.

Opera in the Park (Sept)

This is a very special San Francisco event held every year just before the opera season begins. It takes place in the Bandshell in Golden Gate Park in the afternoon and is free. Hundreds of people stake their places from early morning; they bring along very elaborate picnics and wait for the performance. The singers on opening night affirm their love for the city.

Dickens Fair (Nov/Dec)

The Bay Area is unashamedly fond of ye goode olde times which they import from England and then improvise upon. The Dickens Fair is held annually in winter.

Street Fairs

Showcasing arts and crafts by various neighborhoods at different times of the year: the gay-influenced Castro fair, the hippie Haight-Ashbury one, yuppie Union Street and the distinctly Italian North Beach fair.

Check the **Pink Pages** of the *San Francisco Chronicle* during your stay to see if any of the fairs are taking place. Call ahead to confirm all events listed. Here are the listings for 24-hour current event tape recordings:

San Francisco Visitors Bureau,
Auf Deutsch: 391-2004
En Espanol: 391-2122
En Francais: 391-2003
In Japanese: 291-2101

MUSEUMS

San Francisco offers a variety of unbeatable museum experiences:

The American Carousel Museum, 633 Beach St.; 928-0500.
The museum displays antique carousel animals from 1880 to 1930. There is a restoration room designed to resemble a 1910 carving shop, and demonstrations in restoration techniques are held. Open daily, 10 a.m. - 6 p.m. Check beforehand; the museum has been undergoing extensive restoration.

Cable Car Barn and Museum, 1201 Mason St.; 474-1887.
This 1907 red brick barn is the center for San Francisco's motorless cars.

Go look at the underground workings of the only surviving cable car system in the world, Andrew Hallidie's original Car #8, and vintage photographs. A 16-minute film, *The Cable Car and How It Works,* plays continuously. Open daily, 10 a.m. - 5 p.m., November to March, and until 6 p.m., April to October.

California Crafts Museum, Ghirardelli Square, 900 North Point Road; 771-1919.
The museum displays contemporary crafts of glass, fiber, ceramic, paper, wood and metal. Open daily, noon to 7 p.m., and on Thursday and Friday, until 9 p.m.

Chinese Culture Center, Holiday Inn, 750 Kearny St., 3rd Floor; 986-1822.
Exhibits contemporary Chinese art. The center is open Tuesday to Saturday 10 a.m. - 4 p.m.

Fort Point National Historic Site, Presidio; 556-1693.
Built to accommodate 126 cannon mounts and 600 soldiers, it is the only building on the West Coast that typifies the seacoast fortifications of the 1880s. It was designated a National Historic Site in 1970. National Park Rangers dressed in Civil War period clothing explain the fort's history. Open daily, 10 a.m. - 5 p.m.

Jewish Community Museum, 121 Steuart St.; 543-8880.
The museum is dedicated to exploring the art and culture of the Jewish Community. Exhibitions change frequently and there are lectures and multi-media presentations. Open Monday - Wednesday noon - 6 p.m.; Thursday noon - 8 p.m.; Sunday 10 a.m. - 6 p.m.

Joseph Dee Museum of Photography, 45 Kearny St., Second Floor; 392-1900.
Displays 150 years of photographic history. Both local and national artists are featured in rotating exhibitions. Open weekdays, 9 a.m. - 5 p.m.

Mexican Museum, Fort Mason Center, Bldg. D, Laguna St. and Marina Blvd; 441-0404.
The only such museum in the United States. It features rotating exhibitions of pre-Hispanic and colonial art, folk art, Mexican fine arts and Mexican-American art. Open Wednesday to Sunday, noon - 5 p.m.

Museo Italo Americano, Fort Mason Center, Bldg. C, Laguna St. and Marina Blvd; 673-2200.
Exhibits works by Italians and Italian-Americans with emphasis on contemporary artists. Open Wednesday to Sunday, noon - 5 p.m.

Old Mint Museum, 88 Fifth St.; 774-6830.

This building, opened in 1874, is one of the best examples of federal classical revival architecture in the West. It displays Western art and a collection of pioneer gold coins. The tour includes a film, ore and mineral exhibits as well as gold bars worth millions. Open Monday to Friday, 10 a.m. - 4 p.m.

San Francisco Craft and Folk Art Museum, Fort Mason Center, Bldg. A, Laguna St. and Marina Blvd; 775-0990.

Works loaned by major museums and pieces from private collections are fea-

tured, including contemporary craft pieces. Open Tuesday to Friday, Sunday, 11 a.m. - 5 p.m.; Saturday 10 a.m. - 5 p.m.

San Francisco International Toy Museum, 2801 Leavenworth St.; 441-8697.

Features antique toys from around the world as well as a hands-on exhibit of new toys called "The Play Space". Open Tuesday to Saturday, 10 a.m. - 5 p.m. and Sunday, 11 a.m. - 5 p.m.

Cartoon Art Museum, 665 Third St., Fifth Floor; 546-3922.

Rotating exhibits of cartoon art and artifacts. You can see actual artwork of cartoons for newspapers, magazines and comic books. Open Wednesday to Fri-

day, 11 a.m. - 5 p.m.; Saturday 10 a.m. - 5 p.m.; Sunday 1 p.m. - 5 p.m.

Galleria De La Raza, 2851 24th St.; 826-8009.

Displays work by Chicano and Latino artists. Sponsors cultural events in conjunction with current exhibitions. Open Tuesday to Saturday, noon - 6 p.m.

San Francisco African-American Historical and Cultural Society, Fort Mason, Bldg. C; 441-0640.

The museum offers exhibits as well as organizing its own field trips to relevant and well-known Black historical sites. Open only on Wednesday to Sunday noon - 5 p.m.

San Francisco History Room and Archives, Public Library, Third Floor; 558-3949.

Exhibitions change frequently. It contains a large book and pamphlet collection, photographs and maps. Open Thursday and Saturday, 10 - 6 p.m. and Tuesday, Wednesday and Friday, 1 p.m. - 6 p.m.

Society of California Pioneers, 456 McAllister St.; 861-5278.

Operated by the Society of California Pioneers, it displays 19th-century California paintings. It also has a Children's Gallery featuring Californian history, artifacts from the Gold Rush and costumes. Open Monday to Friday, 10 a.m. - 4 p.m. It is closed during August.

TOURS

The Bay Area offers some unique tours. Even natives go on these interesting and informative excursions. Many take small groups only so you can hear the tour leader.

NB: As soon as you know the tour you wish to take, call the relevant company to ensure a place. Some, like the Sentimental Tours, are booked weeks in advance.

By Air

Commodore Helicopters, 240 Redwood Highway, Highway 101, Mill Valley, 332-4482.

Spectacular tours of the bay, Golden Gate Bridge and the city skyline, ranging from 7 to 60 miles (11 to 96 km). Wine country and other charters available upon advance request.

San Francisco Helicopter Tours, 1-800-400-2404 or 510-632-9422.

Daily flights that depart from the Oakland airport for tours of the Bay, the wine country, the coast of Monterey and to other Bay Area destinations. Pickup service is available from San Francisco hotels.

Sentimental Journeys Sky Tours/Charters, North Field, Oakland International Airport, 667-3800, 1-800-634-1165.

This tour will appeal to flying buffs. Relive the golden days of air travel aboard a DC-3. Drinks and *hors d'oeuvres* will be served as you fly past the Golden Gate Bridge, Alcatraz, Fisherman's Wharf, the Marin Coastline etc.

Walking Tours

Café Walks, 355 24th Avenue, 751-4286.

Enjoy an unusual and personalized introduction to San Francisco by walking through neighborhoods such as North Beach, Pacific Heights, the Marina, the Financial District, Haight-Ashbury and the Richmond. Judith Kahn's tours are two-and-a-half-hour strolls which include refreshments and stops at various cafés.

Introduction to San Francisco: Helen's Walk Tour, P.O. Box 9164, Berkeley, 94709, 510-524-4544.

Helen's Walk is for anyone who would like to be a San Franciscan for a day. There are five plans to choose from: Fisherman's Wharf, North Beach, Chinatown and Victorian Mansions, with the Grand Tour being a combination of the first three. The number of people in a group is limited to keep the tour personalized. French, Arabic and Spanish tours are available. Every tour includes a cable car ride.

Friends of Recreation and Parks, McLaren Lodge, Stanyan and Fell Streets, Golden Gate Park, 221-1311.

Guides offer thorough tours of the park, pointing out the flora, fauna and history. Free. From May - October, Saturday, 11 a.m. and Sunday, 11 a.m. and 2 p.m.

Cruisin' the Castro, 550-8110.

Trevor Hailey, the tour guide, has been a member of the gay community for the past 15 years and escorts you on an informative tour of the Castro, the heart of San Francisco's gay community. Learn about Harvey Milk, the first gay elected into politics in the U.S., visit the home of the Names Project, discover book stores and gift shops. Tours start daily at 10 a.m. and are limited (reservation only) to 16 people. They include a stop at the Patio Café restaurant for lunch during the week and for breakfast on weekends.

The City Guides, Friends of the San Francisco Library, Main Library, Civic Center, 558-3981.

A city guide will give you a lively and anecdotal tour of the city's history, architecture and culture. These free tours are scheduled throughout the week. No reservations required, just call up for times of departure.

Chinatown Walking Tours with Wok Wiz, P.O. Box 1583, Pacifica 94044, 355-9657.

Shirley Fong-Torres is a well-known cookbook author and restaurant critic who provides an illuminating look into Chinatown during the tour. You will be given historical information and will get an opportunity to visit back alleys, a herbal shop, a fortune cookie factory and a Chinese bakery among other places. Finish the tour with dim sum at a popular teahouse. Abbreviated, 90-minute tours; reservations required.

Shopping Tours

Shop till you drop, 344-2120.

Two shopping pros give tours tailored to your every need and taste. They will even take you out of town.

ARTS/PHOTO CREDITS

Photography	**David Ryan** *and*
Cover (Houghton Mifflin)	**Dallas & John Heaton**
Front Cover (Apa & GeoCenter)	**Ben Nakayama**
Back Cover (Apa & GeoCenter)	**David Ryan**
14/15	**Apa Photo Agency**
48	**Lee Foster**
Maps	**Berndtson & Berndtson**
Cover Design and Handwriting	**V. Barl**

INSIGHT GUIDES

COLORSET NUMBERS

You'll find the colorset number on the spine of each Insight Guide.

INSIGHT *POCKET* GUIDES

• •

United States: **Houghton Mifflin Company, Boston MA 02108**
Tel: (800) 2253362 Fax: (800) 4589501

Canada: **Thomas Allen & Son, 390 Steelcase Road East**
Markham, Ontario L3R 1G2
Tel: (416) 4759126 Fax: (416) 4756747

Great Britain: **GeoCenter UK, Hampshire RG22 4BJ**
Tel: (256) 817987 Fax: (256) 817988

Worldwide: **Höfer Communications Singapore 2262**
Tel: (65) 8612755 Fax: (65) 8616438

66 I was first drawn to the Insight Guides by the excellent "Nepal" volume. I can think of no book which so effectively captures the essence of a country. Out of these pages leaped the Nepal I know – the captivating charm of a people and their culture. I've since discovered and enjoyed the entire Insight Guide Series. Each volume deals with a country or city in the same sensitive depth, which is nowhere more evident than in the superb photography. 99

Sir Edmund Hillary

NOTES

NOTES